D.E.B.T.

Free or Die Trying

SECOND EDITION

By
Marcus Garrett

READ THIS FIRST

As a thank you for purchasing, I'm giving away a free pdf of the wealth-building system I implemented after getting out of debt: *The Playbook: From $30,000 in Debt to Six Figure Wealth*. Fill out the form at TheMarcusGarrett.com to have it sent directly to your inbox.

"I share **<u>systems</u>** that help people decrease their debt and increase their wealth."

Paychecks and Balances, LLC

"We help working professionals make money, save money, get out of debt, and build wealth."

Disclaimer

The information contained within this book is strictly for educational purposes. If you wish to apply ideas contained in this book, you are taking full responsibility for your actions.

The author has made every effort to ensure the accuracy of the information within this book was correct at time of publication. The author does not assume and hereby disclaims any liability to any party for any loss, damage, or disruption caused by errors or omissions, whether such errors or omissions result from accident, negligence, or any other cause.

This information is provided and sold with the knowledge that the publisher and author do not offer any legal or other professional advice. Should the need arise for any such expertise, the reader should consult with the appropriate professional.

This book does not contain all the information available on the subject. This book has not been created to be specific to any individual's or organization's situation or needs. Every effort has been made to make this book as accurate as possible. However, there may be typographical and/or content errors. Therefore, this book should serve only as a general guide and not as the ultimate source of subject information.

The author and publisher shall have no liability or responsibility to any person or entity regarding any loss or damage incurred, or alleged to have incurred, directly or indirectly, by the information contained in this book.

Dedication and Appreciation

I would like to dedicate this book to everyone who refuses to give up.

I also want to thank all the people in my life, far too many to name individually, for their help and support. Specifically, thank you to my mother and father, family, and close friends. Without your love, support, and mentorship, I know I would have never succeeded. I cannot thank you all enough. I love you.

In the realm of financial support, I thank all my past and present employers who have gainfully employed me since the age of 16. My gratitude continues despite the regret some of you may feel in hindsight. Without you, I would not have managed to be a mostly honest tax-paying citizen who climbed out of debt and who occasionally had the discretionary income to enjoy dessert wine while keeping my light bill paid.

Thank you to the editor of this revised edition for making it better than ever! You can find her at janalynch.me or on Twitter (@saysjana).

Foreword

And now a message from J.D. Roth of GetRichSlowly.org.

I spent my twenties paying interest. And my thirties.

For two decades, I was mired in consumer debt: credit cards, car loans, computer loans, home-equity loans, a loan from my *wife* — even a loan from my wife's grandmother! I was miserable with money and money was miserable to me.

Oh, how I wish I'd had a book like this thirty years ago. Instead, I stumbled in the dark seeking answers. I didn't find any.

You're more fortunate than I was. You *do* have this book. Here you'll find the answers you need to get out of debt — and stay out of debt.

If you too have been stumbling in the dark, desperately seeking some sort of salvation, Marcus Garrett is here to lead you to the light. Like me, he's been there. He's been where you are. As you'll learn in the first half of *Debt Free or Die Trying*, he's a graduate from the School of Hard Knocks. He's made mistakes (as have we all) and he's had bad stuff happen to him (as have we all).

"In one weekend, I nearly tripled my debt," Marcus writes. "I didn't know it then, but I would spend the greater part of the next eight years paying off debt I accumulated in less than eight hours." *Ouch.*

The good news is that Marcus got his shit together. It took time and toil, but he repaid his debt. Along the way, he learned a thing or two about how money works. Now you get the reap the rewards of his hard-won wisdom.

Marcus has reduced his advice to four simple steps:

- Define the problem.
- Establish a plan.
- Build a budget.
- Trust the process.

But while these steps are simple, they're not easy.

It's not difficult to dig yourself into debt; it takes more effort to fill in the hole. But if you don't pick up the shovel, who will? If you don't start today, when will you? How much worse do things need to get before you decide to act?

Your first step to a debt-free future is to read this book and put its ideas into action.

Define the problem. Establish a plan. Build a budget. Trust the process.

Do these things and you *will* achieve that debt-free life you've always dreamed of. I did. Marcus did. You can too.

TABLE OF CONTENTS

Introduction

I like to believe the advice I recommend is relevant to everyone, but to manage expectations, please keep the following in mind:

- **Unmarried**—When I wrote this book, I was unmarried. And for the majority, of my debt-freedom journey I was single. At various times, I was in committed relationships with women who in roughly equal parts helped decrease or increase my debt. However, this book is not focused on how others helped or harmed my goals of living debt-free. I believe you can get out of debt while in a relationship, but it will take a far more concerted effort to get two people aligned with an already difficult pursuit.

- **No Children**—Children add an additional variable and expense that I can neither comment on nor directly relate to beyond my experience dating women with children of their own. However, I believe the general ideas covered in this book are sound whether you have children or not.

- **Investments**—Because this book focuses on my debt-freedom journey, I won't discuss much about investments. I have had - and continue to have - various investments, none of which bias my opinions on tips and strategies for debt management. I make no recommendations on the best or worst options for allocating or managing your debts or where to invest your money (or with whom). I recommend you do your due diligence and choose the apps, software, or investment and debt- management strategies best aligned with your goals.

- **Transportation**—I figure this area is minor but worth mentioning. Although I owned a car while originally writing this book, I paid it off in 2010 (I cover how I accomplished this later in the book). During the bulk of my debt- repayment journey, I primarily relied on public transportation[1] This greatly reduced my transportation costs, and for this reason, beyond car loan payments, this book does not comprehensively address the cost of owning a car.

For those of you who read the first edition (thank you), I decided to update this book for a few reasons. I got older, seven years to be exact, and allegedly, I should be wiser.[2] In 2018, I set a goal to read and review the 15 best personal finance and investment books at PaychecksAndBalances.com/Books. In order of my favorites:

1. Debt Free or Die Trying by Marcus Garrett
2. The Millionaire Next Door: The Surprising Secrets of America's Wealthy by Thomas J. Stanley
3. The Automatic Millionaire by David Bach
4. I Will Teach You To Be Rich by Ramit Sethi
5. Rich Dad Poor Dad by Robert Kiyosaki
6. A Random Walk Down Wall Street by Burton Malkiel
7. The Dos and Don'ts of Money: Easy Solutions for Everyday Problems by Suze Orman

---

[1] Why this matters: the three largest expenses, accounting for 60 to 70 percent of the average household budget, are housing (33%) and transportation (16%), food-related expenses (13%).

[2] This is subject to debate, but for the purposes of this revision, we'll assume it is accurate.

8. The Total Money Makeover by Dave Ramsey

9. The Two-Income Trap: Why Middle-Class Parents are Going Broke by Elizabeth Warren

10. Dollars and Sense by Dan Ariely and Jeff Kreisler

11. Your Money or Your Life by Vicki Robin, Joe Dominguez, Monique Tilford

12. Your Credit Score: How to Improve the 3-Digit Number that Shapes Your Financial Future by Liz Weston

13. The Richest Man in Babylon by George Samuel Clason

14. Irrational Exuberance by Robert Shiller

15. The Intelligent Investor by Benjamin Graham

These reads, coupled with a dash of Millennial vanity, led to the update you are reading today. And as you have noticed by now, my book is a short read that focuses exclusively on debt. That is a purposeful choice.

To supplement what I discuss, I will refer to books from the list above or other personal finance books I believe take a deeper dive into the topic covered. Overall, I have tried to make this edition better, more instructional, and added specific *Calls to Action* based on my own failures and wins with money and in life.

Interwoven with my own personal experiences with debt and money mismanagement, this revised book outlines these four talking points in much greater detail and hopefully, with much better delivery than my permanently archived televised interview. Throughout the book, you will read painful money lessons that should serve as warnings. When unclear, I will specifically call these red flags out. I highly recommend you avoid them in your life.

I've added a clear list of *Calls to Action* (**CTA**) at the end of each chapter. These will help you avoid reaching rock bottom, or at least allow you to see the warning signs on your way there. I hope you learn something meaningful from my experiences and enjoy *D.E.B.T. Free or Die Trying* (Second Edition).

The Origin Story: D.E.B.T. Free

In 2018, I was preparing for an on-air interview with a local CBS News affiliate. This was my second interview with them, but this time I wouldn't have the benefit of a panel to play off or field questions I had no idea how to answer. I had to sink or swim on my own.

Before the interview, a producer asked me to send in my talking points. I was flattered they assumed[3] I had a plan. I later learned that these would be used for their on-screen graphics.

Given that I had approximately zero media training, I had no idea what to provide. However, I *had* worked as an auditor for over a decade. This experience sufficiently prepared me for making boring presentations on live TV, so I planned to do the exact opposite of what I did every day.

With this work experience haunting my subconscious, I decided to go completely off script and blurted out an acronym I thought might keep the make-believe Millennial I created in my head from falling asleep on their couch. With pretend grace and eloquence, I managed to summarize my book into four easy steps that from that point forward would be referred to as "D.E.B.T." Free.

---

[3] Incorrectly.

D.E.B.T. FREE:
4 Week Starter Kit

D. = Define the problem
E. = Establish a plan
B. = Build a budget
T. = Trust the process

PAYCHECKS
&BALANCES

Chapter 1
How I Buried Myself $30,000 in Debt

In America, getting into debt is comically easy. You're only one credit-card-fueled night out, badly planned investment, extended hospital stay, or loan-funded college education away from thousands of dollars of debt.

If you're reading this book, you probably already know.

If you're a baller, this is no big deal. If you're a non-baller like me, a few thousand dollars in debt is a very big deal.

It can derail your entire life.

My battle with debt derailed about a decade of my life.

Like most financially irresponsible people of my generation, I got my first credit card when I was 18 years old. I didn't know anything about credit cards. I didn't know much about money management, either. But, like many 18-year-olds, I thought I knew a lot.

I was wrong.

My naivety combined with my arrogance made me the perfect target. I was young and ignorant yet legally old enough to make contractually obligated purchases that were impulsive and irresponsible. I was a credit card company's ideal customer.

The credit card companies represented on my college campus during freshman orientation sure thought that. I had a job, but I didn't make a lot of money and I didn't have a lot of disposable income. The representatives didn't seem to mind; they believed I should own multiple credit cards.

They were right, too, and I had about 10 credit cards before I was legally old enough to drink. I vividly remember signing up for my first credit card the way you do most tragic events in your life. I was walking through my dorm's community area, and a guy asked if I wanted a free T-shirt. A free T-shirt? HELL YEAH.

To get it, I had to sign up for something called a "credit card." No big deal, right? After all, the (very long) line was filled with my peers. I assumed that if everyone else was lining up for this thing, it couldn't be that bad.

We were sheep. I often wonder how my other free T-shirt-clad peers fared in the game of debt. I hope they made out better than I did.

But I digress. Back to the story of my first credit card.

When I applied, I had a debit card and the possession of this made me, in my mind, a financial expert. My expertise convinced me, uncorrected by the credit card company representative, that credit cards were free money. Banks gave it to you, and all you had to do was pay back a minimal amount at the end of each month.

In my 18-year-old mind, it seemed like a steal.

As I was filling out the paperwork for my first card, the guy helpfully explained that several areas weren't important, and I didn't need to bother filling them out. That should have set off alarms. But I was 18. I didn't care about contracts, and I sure didn't care enough to read them. Not when I had to make the life-changing decision between a free T-shirt, yo-yo, or Frisbee.

So, I filled out what they told me I absolutely had to, collected my T-shirt emblazoned with the logo of a company I'm certain has since filed for bankruptcy and a yo-yo. I then promptly forgot about the whole incident until weeks later.

I didn't know it at the time, but years of experience have taught me that credit cards show up like something mailed to you from the National Security Agency. It's all very top secret. I appreciate their thinly veiled attempts to hide my credit card from would-be thieves, which I assume is to ensure that only *I* can cause contractually irreparable harm to my financial well-being.[4]

Having completely forgotten the ordeal of applying for a credit card, I had no clue what might be inside that ominous-looking envelope. In hindsight, that should have been red flag number one because that windowless envelope contained the worst thing - financially speaking - to ever happen to me.

Inside, I found an all-black credit card.

Do not confuse this with the American Express Black Card. That Black Card is given only to people who can afford things I only fantasize about while waiting in line to buy lottery tickets.

This was a black-colored card, a credit card given to ignorant college students with minimal income and maximum material aspirations.

I didn't realize the impact of being awarded my first credit card. I also grossly underestimated the impact it would have on my life. And, once again, I did not read the contract.

---

[4] It is not like anyone with foul intentions would ever open an anonymous envelope emblazoned with the words 'do not open.'

I called the number on the attached sticker to activate it, placed it in my wallet, and moved on with whatever activity 18-year-old men engaged in for the '99 and the 2000s.[5]

Weeks, or possibly months, passed before I used my credit card. I can't remember the first purchase, but I want to believe it was for something reasonable, like food, water, or 22-inch rims.

Like many people now burdened with thousands of dollars of debt, I started simple enough. I'd buy something I wanted here or there on credit even though I was perfectly capable of paying cash. I justified using the card by assuring myself I'd pay off the balance in full as soon as the bill arrived. But when I saw how low the eye-popping "minimum payment"[6] was I couldn't bring myself to pay more.

> *DFDT Tip: The typical "minimum payment" is calculated as a percentage of your principal (total balance). This may be as low as 2-percent.*
>
> *For instance, a $10,000 total balance would have a monthly minimum payment of **only** $200. However, paying only the minimum payment on a $10,000 balance with an APR of 15% would take you over 30 years for total costs of about $25,573. $15,573 of this would be interest paid.*

I mean, I wasn't a total idiot. "Let the banks take all the risk" was a common refrain, and I told myself that the next time was when I'd pay the balance in full. And it was always next time.

Surprisingly, during my first few years of credit card ownership, I didn't make any substantial purchases. I never bought much

---

[5] Probably rhythmic shuffling to the soulful sounds of "Whoomph There It Is." It was a simpler time back then.

[6] I like bankrate.com/calculators for estimating credit card payments plus interest.

that cost more than a few dollars. However, it's amazing how even minor purchases, coupled with astronomical APR rates, can add up. Soon, all those one-off purchases from month to month added up to hundreds of dollars, which eventually grew to thousands of dollars.

Still, it seemed like no matter how high my outstanding balance became, my minimum payment remained low. This low monthly payment was quite a victory in my young mind. I thought I was winning, and the banks were losing in this game of financial chess.

Over time, I started getting more and more credit card offers, which I eagerly accepted. I mean, who could resist those "zero percent APR" and "zero percent balance transfer" slogans?

> *DFDT Tip: Expect your "zero percent balance" transfer to last 12, 18, or up to 24 months. Be sure to write this in your smartphone or personal calendar. In most instances, there will be no formal warning prior to your interest rate increasing to the new APR rate (reflected in the transfer contract agreement you probably didn't read 12, 18, or 24 months earlier).*

I couldn't. And before long, I had three or four major credit cards on top of the two or three my college credit card pals had signed me up for on my first day of school. I read somewhere – probably on the Internet[7] – that you shouldn't cancel credit cards, so as a financially savvy, up-and-coming expert of the world, I would

---

[7] There is some logic to this reasoning. A basic breakdown of your credit score includes: Payment History: 35 percent; Debt Ratio (how much you owe compared to your available credit limit): 30 percent; Credit History (age of credit usage): 15 percent; New Credit: 10 percent; Mix of Various Types of Credit: 10 percent.

open new credit card accounts anytime a better offer arrived in the mail.

Smart, right? I knew what I was doing. But, despite the magnitude of my irresponsibility, I've only ever missed one credit card payment. That's jumping ahead in the story, though.

The first couple of years went smoothly. From 18 to 20, I only racked up a few thousand dollars in debt. I didn't really start hitting the big-time debt numbers until I became roommates with an old high school friend.

Don't get me wrong. It wasn't his fault. He *always* paid his half of the rent. This is not a compliment I can pay most roommates I've had.

I do, however, attribute some blame to my apartment complex, which introduced me to the customer-friendly opportunity of making rent payments via credit card.

In the race to capitalize on the financially ignorant, our apartment managers were light-years ahead of their time.[8]

Although I had some recollection of how to be responsible with money from the time before credit cards, I thought the idea that my apartment managers accepting credit cards for rent payment was nothing short of a blessing from the Almighty himself. I knew, in theory, I was supposed to maintain a cash budget and my multiple credit cards were supposed to be used for "emergency."

However, what defines an emergency at age 20 versus any age that isn't 20 is subjective. As I signed my apartment's 12-month

---

[8] In fairness, I can't speak to how other apartment managers worked. For me, accepting credit cards for rent payment was the equivalent of Saint Peter asking me if I want to cut in line at the gates of Heaven.

contract with my roommate, rent-on-credit sounded perfectly practical. Reality, on the other hand, unfolded a little differently.

In the beginning, paying my rent with my credit card was the exception, rather than the rule.[9]Soon, I found it increasingly difficult to justify paying rent with my hard-earned money while my credit cards sat idle.

Every month I charged my rent to my credit card while promising myself that it would be the last time. And, despite not having any additional income to support this fantasy, I told myself I would repay myself. You can imagine how well that went. Eventually I got tired of lying to myself and completely gave up on the idea.

Instead, I told myself that I was going to college and when I graduated and was a big baller, I would pay off my debt in a couple of months. I justified my flawed logic by telling myself *You Only Live Once!* and other similar clichés. These somehow convinced the younger me that once I graduated from college I would be *Balling Out of Control*, and would be able to pay back these nominal expenditures in *The Blink of an Eye* because *It Is What It Is*.

With the pesky restrictions of responsibility completely shed, I finally allowed myself to freely *Make it Rain!* …on credit.

You might be surprised to learn that I did have a job at this time. My job involved completing catalog orders in a call center for $9 an hour, but I'm sure I had a grandiose title worthy of my financial expenditures like *Telephone Payment Compilation Scientist*. Not that it mattered because I used my credit cards to pay for anything, I didn't feel like paying for in cash. For clarity, this meant I paid for *everything* with credit.

---

[9] The "beginning" is defined here as a short period of time that unfortunately is nowhere as encompassing and close to "towards the end."

To make matters better (or worse), I'd also apply the same logic to my friends' expenses. If they didn't have a means to pay, I used my credit cards to fill the gap between the lifestyle I should have been living and the lifestyle we wanted to live.

Naturally, this extended to any woman, or women,[10] I dated.

Demonstrating my appreciation for the finer things in life, I decided to put a loud bass system in my car. No used car of mine would be complete without equally tasteful waist-high chrome rims to accentuate my credit-funded sound system.

> One example that captures the opulent spending of my youth might or might not involve a long, expensive, poorly planned road trip to the NBA All-Star weekend in Atlanta my sophomore year of college. In short, I turned $20 in cash into $1000 of debt, a ton of miles on my car, and a cautionary tale of what can happen when a 20-year-old wants to impress some friends and live above his means.
>
> The NBA All-Star weekend came to Atlanta my sophomore year of college, and my friends and I decided we had to go. Doing anything else, like study for the midterms we all had coming up, made so little sense to us that going on an impromptu road trip didn't even warrant a group debate. We had to go to the NBA All-Star game. Since we attended different schools, we made plans to meet in Austin, Texas, before making the 13-hour road trip to Atlanta, Georgia. We were too young to rent a car, but one of our older friends agreed to sign over the rental car if we promised to be responsible.

---

[10] (usually women)

She clearly overestimated our capacity to meet this promise, but nevertheless her misplaced trust was our gain.

The week of the trip, I realized I only had $20 cash on hand, which, given my income management skills at the time, was pretty good. A wiser man, or even someone who wasn't a complete idiot, might have abstained from the trip upon realizing his weekend budget was limited to three McDonald's Happy Meals. Young me, however, lacked that kind of insight and wisdom. I simply decided that anything beyond $20 would go on any one of my many credit cards, which I had somehow managed not to max out.

My inability, but not lack of will, to max out my cards probably had to do with the fact that each month brought more credit card offers and more credit limit increases. In fact, by this point, I had at least $10,000-$15,000 in available credit extended to me.

Coincidentally, my credit limits always seemed to increase right when I needed to buy or do something, I had no business buying or doing. It's as if the credit card companies had an algorithm synchronized with my financial stupidity. Our trip to Atlanta was no exception.

Between my three friends and me, we were lucky if we had $53 in total cash. On the bright side, one of our friends had family in Atlanta, so we only needed gas money – plus food and water, if you want to split hairs. We set out on the 13-hour drive, promptly driving in the wrong direction for four of

> those hours before self-correcting on the newly estimated 16-hour, one-day trip. The rest, as they say, is history.
>
> I can't lie. It was a great trip! For legal and moral purposes, I can't discuss all the details, and it's not as if I remember 80% of them anyway. Even if I did, I would deny it. What I do know and will admit is that I left Austin with approximately $2,000 in credit card debt and I returned to Austin with about $3,000 in credit card debt. You might balk at the idea that I mysteriously spent $1,000 in credit and $20 in cash in a single weekend, but I assure you that 20-something me felt this was money (and credit) well spent.

This credit card spending binge is one of many examples of my inability to care about how much money I spent, if it was spent on credit. I never thought about how much debt I was accumulating. It seemed like no matter what I bought; the minimum payments were always manageable. And if the minimum payments were manageable, 20-something me assumed everything was fine.

This flawed mindset would haunt me for years. My ability to ignore my growing debt was so easy that I literally never thought about it.

Why?

Because most of my debt was accumulated in small purchases rather than the more obvious gigantic ones. Save for the occasional credit-financed road trip, I was somehow self-conscious enough not to make large purchases.

However, there is one very large and very expensive exception to this.

Before the perils of texting while driving were turned into TV commercials and billboards, I was a chronic text-driver. During one particularly passionate text-driving incident, I took my eyes off the road for what seemed like a moment. However, since this was pre-smartphones, I did so on a 10-key Nokia phone. It's possible I took my eyes off the road for an entire 24-hour period since I was texting in QWERTY but it was most likely closer to 15 minutes.

You can probably guess what happened. And if you thought it involved an accident with two flat tires, a series of incredibly stupid (probably too stupid to admit publicly) decisions and choices, and thousands of dollars on credit cards for repairs, you'd be correct.

It also involved some tears and me finally—FINALLY—realizing that I was in DEBT.

> Before my eyes returned to the road, I was suddenly careening into the median. However, I wouldn't exactly describe what transpired as a "wreck." That would give too much credit to the ignorance of the situation. Fortunately, I was able to self-correct before I did any major damage to my or any other vehicle. What I did manage to do was flatten both tires on the driver's side. My car nearly disabled, I willed it to a side street before running completely out of options.
>
> I had two choices now.
>
> There was the logical first choice: I could call my parents, who had access to AAA, and explain the situation. I'd likely receive a lecture and possibly have my car taken away. Not ideal, but practical.

Then there was the illogical second choice: I could call my friend who did not have AAA or any money but who would provide moral and logistical support, and, while he may laugh at my plight, he would not lecture or take my car away. Please note that this incident predated social media, so his smart remarks would be limited to my face versus Myspace or Facebook. In later years, the possibility of being made fun of in person and on social media may have weighed heavily on my final decision. So, using the same cell phone that had gotten me into this predicament, I called my friend.

Before he arrived, I managed to replace one of the tires with a spare and decreased my dumbass, self-inflicted problem by 50%. A generously empathetic person might call this progress. And to my credit, it was. But my financial decision making in this situation was very telling. Because the only thing more nonsensical than what you'll justify spending money on in your 20s is what you won't spend money on. In my case, it was something as simple as a tow truck.

Despite spending thousands of dollars on mundane material objects that had no appreciable value, I balked at my friend's suggestion to call a tow truck because that was, as I described it to him, "[expletive] expensive." I became convinced that I could drive my impaired vehicle to a local repair shop that I used before because I had also convinced myself that my repeat business meant that they would rip me off slightly less than many of the other, closer repair shops. My friend, loyalty unquestioned, agreed to follow me the 10 or so miles it would take to get to the repair shop with his hazard lights on to prevent me from being rear-ended, while simultaneously sacrificing his own vehicle for said rear-ending as I drove somewhere between a slug and a snail's pace to prevent my flattened tires from coming completely off the rims before I arrived. A few hours into what should have been a 10-minute drive, we made it to the repair shop. That's where the real fun began.

After a brief diagnosis, the repair shop informed me that they estimated the damages to the vehicle were somewhere in the thousands. They couldn't say for sure because they had no idea how much labor it would take to un-mangle my currently mangled axel and rims. The tone of his voice was a measure of disbelief and confusion. In all his years as a mechanic, he said had never seen the result of something so dim-witted. I like to imagine my repair remains one of the top legends he regales to his mechanic friends over drinks when they talk about the "craziest repairs they ever saw."

Once again, I was faced with two choices. I could call my parents, who might or might not (but likely not) help me with the costly repairs, take my car away and/or give me a lecture, or I could charge the whole thing to my multiple, near-maxed out credit cards, regardless of cost, and take this story with me to my grave (or now, until my parents read this book). To the surprise of no one, I chose the second option.

This situation made me swear off credit cards for good, temporarily. I didn't want to keep adding to my debt. And, amazingly, I would be responsible for some time before completely forgetting the lesson I learned.

****

Spring semester of my sophomore year of college, I randomly decided I had enough of the University of Texas-Austin.[11]

My parents put up surprisingly little protest to the idea They only had two qualifiers:

1. It couldn't cost them any additional money; and

2. I didn't drop out of school.

I had no plans to drop out of school. But I completely understand why my parents thought I would. My GPA and general inability to maintain a full course load for a complete semester before deciding it was "too much to handle" a few weeks into each semester gave them no reason to believe otherwise. In my defense, I did manage to hold down steady jobs in college. For the most part, I even showed up to some of my classes.[12]

I just didn't prepare before I got there, try hard once I arrived, or study after I left. Besides these minor limitations, I was a model student.

In the summer of 2003 at the ripe old age of 21, I took my model student behavior and randomly selected another university to attend. My criteria for picking my next school?

---

[11] It is only now, with the benefit of years, that I acknowledge I left because I was too lazy for schoolwork and lacked commitment to academic success.

[12] If I found them interesting, and they started after 9:00 a.m. or when I woke up, whichever came later.

It needed to be a public university covered by the program my parents used to help pay for public school. I wasn't about to use my credit cards for educational purposes!

Solid standards, right?

In the end, I chose Sam Houston State University (SHSU). Honestly, I was scared the city of Houston was too close to my family and friends. At least I had the foresight to accept that I didn't have the mental discipline necessary to attend college in the same ZIP code as my equally irresponsible peers. I was perfectly capable of reckless negligence on my own.

With minimal transfer paperwork and a summer break, I was officially SHSU- bound.

Unfortunately, changing schools didn't change my thoughts, behavior, or habits. I remained convinced that once I finished college, I would get a job balling so hard that my college debt wouldn't matter. And to this day, I do not know why I thought a college education entitled me to a huge annual income. While I'm aware of the correlation between education and income, I can assure you it is nothing like the one I made up in my head.

> *DFDT Tip: Almost half of millennials said their biggest mistake was overestimating the salary of their first post-college job and assuming they could afford monthly payments, according to a 2019 SoFi survey.*

I thought if you didn't know how to rap or weren't athletically gifted — two areas where I, unfortunately, failed to excel — then college was the next best "get-rich- quick" scheme. As a result, during college, I was never particularly concerned about how much debt I was accumulating nor did I ever make a concerted effort to start paying off my credit cards.

Have you ever watched a poorly scripted movie? A movie where one second, everything makes sense and then the next minute you're completely lost? That pretty much sums up what happened to me and my debt during the last two years of college.

One year, I was a mere few thousand dollars in debt.[13] Then - bam! Twelve months pass and I'm tens of thousands of dollars in debt. And I had no idea how it happened. It's as if I went to sleep with some semblance of responsibility and woke up indebted. I can't recall all the individual activities, but there is one that still haunts my subconscious (and wallet).

This story involves me, friends, and some very, very poor financial decision making. Except this time, it took place on South Padre Island, Texas, during spring break. If nothing else, at least I like to switch up the locations of my financial mishaps. I'm fancy like that.

> **Spring break South Padre Island, Texas**—For those of you who are not familiar with this college experience, spring break is an American-themed holiday which I believe originates from farmer times when kids had to return home to help their families till the land. While most Americans no longer till farmland, for whatever reason, spring break continues to exist.
>
> Spring break, as I remember it, was a seven-day exodus that allowed my friends and me to reunite and cram our already impressively reckless behavior into 168 continuous hours of wild activities and unchaperoned moral debauchery. Since I didn't have much cash at the time — because, as a reminder, I paid for everything on

---

[13] All from my moderately, yet reasonably, irresponsible endeavors.

credit, lived check-to-check, and was generally careless with any leftover amount of money I might have been able to save — I put almost all of my spring break excursions and related expenses on my credit cards. In principle, this meant approximately each year I bulk-spent several thousand dollars on hotels, rental cars, alcohol, and other miscellaneous, yet equally dumb, purchases because I felt it was my personal responsibility to ensure my friends, my friends' friends, and I all had the best seven-day spring break vacations of all time.

Don't get me wrong, folks. I love spring break! Most college kids, including myself, only attended college for the official (and unofficial) breaks, not limited to spring. Everything may have a price, but the price limit for carelessness is infinite.

In a lot of ways, I only know spring break took place because there are plenty of photos documenting my physical presence, even if I was mentally absent. That said, there is no debating the fact that these trips — and others like them — cost me several thousand dollars. Unfortunately, all I have to show for them are blurred memories. There are no assets. No investments. There will be no return on the amount of alcohol and other mostly legal activities I engaged in with my friends in the future except for perhaps acute liver damage. I don't regret the decisions I made in my past, but I do regret how they negatively impacted my future.

But maybe that's how life works.

Chapter 2
Rock Bottom

Seriously, though, I wish I could accurately describe all the ways I managed to increase my debt load over 600 percent in less than three years. Trust that I have tried. In some ways, this budget-amnesia represents the impact not having a budget, or even knowing how much money you spend or owe, can have on your lifestyle. It's hard, perhaps even impossible, to address a problem you don't recognize exists.

Compounding the problem was the fact that, for a long time, I was able to make all the minimum payments. Out of nowhere—at least in my head—I suddenly began to struggle just to make the minimum payments.

Eventually, the financial situation became so bad that by my senior year of college, I began post-dating checks (something I later found out had zero impact on when they were cashed) and mailing checks my checking account lacked the funds to cover. I hoped they wouldn't arrive at the credit card company before my direct deposit hit my account.

Most weeks I got lucky.

Other times, I would open new credit cards just for the "low introductory rates" and transfer payments from one credit card to buy myself a "free" month of not making a credit card payment.

I was slowly becoming a professional debt shuffler. Instead of robbing Peter to pay Paul, I managed to rob myself while paying someone else at double the interest rate. I convinced myself, again, that if I paid the minimum amount each month, by any means necessary, I was ahead of the game.

I was burying myself deeper and deeper in debt.

Perhaps the only thing more troubling than the false reality I had created for myself was the fact that I somehow never had trouble obtaining new credit. From ages 18 to 22, I was never turned down for a credit card. In fact, in my entire life, I've only been turned down for one credit card or loan offer and that was only due to a to a fraudulent charge on my credit report.

Through a miracle, God, luck, or all the above, I was able to keep my debt-shuffling sham going until I finished college. I graduated in 2005 with a degree in business administration and a little less than $10,000 in total consumer debt. A college diploma owner now, all I had to do was show this priceless piece of paper to a few employers and they would obviously agree to pay me six figures for all my effort.

I figured the hardest part was behind me.

In my mind, the obvious next steps were to get rich, pay off my debt, get married, and have a few kids. The most difficult decision I would ever face after college was whether I wanted a one- or two-story home.

I was mistaken.

The worst part of what would become a decade-long struggle with debt hadn't even begun. Until I stepped out into the post-college world, I only thought I had problems.

****

At age 22, I thought a bachelor's degree entitled me to riches. Employers didn't share my grandiose personal assessment. My first job out of college started at less than $20,000.

And I was happy to make that amount!

It took over three months to get a call back from an employer after college. I appreciated my employment, but my ego was devastated. I spent the last four years of my life earning a degree so I could make $9.00 per hour, or about $2.00 per hour more than I was making before I graduated. Technically, I made more money in tips as a waiter, and that job paid me $2.13 an hour!

I was grateful to have any work. Yet, this wasn't exactly the "dream job" I imagined when I sat alone in my room. Yet as I stared at the wall, in the back of my mind I heard my conscious call that I need a job.

Instead of "making it rain," P. Diddy White Parties, and weekend sabbaticals, I had saddled myself with almost $10,000 in debt, and I barely made enough money to cover my monthly minimum credit card payments. For this reason, I moved back in with my parents shortly after graduation. Other than college breaks, I hadn't lived at home full-time in almost five years. I can't speak for my parents but for me, the situation was not ideal.

I was miserable.

As I struggled to fix my life, I became increasingly depressed. Why wasn't I balling out of control? Why was I living at home? Why wasn't anyone ready to show me the money?

This didn't make any sense! Someone had made a terrible mistake. They needed to correct it. You would think during this time that I would have learned to live within my means, make a financial plan, and focus on getting out of debt as soon as possible so I could move forward with my life.

I admire your optimism.

You would be mistaken.

Like any logical person, I wanted to get out of debt. In fact, I had concocted the best-laid plans during those first few months out of college: I'd live at home for a few years[14] while paying off all my debt.

It was the perfect plan, but as it has a habit of doing, real life intervened. First, my parents and I drove each other completely insane. Not only that, they wanted me to pay rent. The audacity of charging me to live in a home I lived in rent-free for 18 years of my life.

In my mind, this was like charging prisoners rent to stay in jail. I didn't even want to live at home! Why would I pay rent to stay there?

My parents had a different outlook. Although years passed before they admitted it to me, they decided it was in everyone's best

---

[14] A plan I can neither confirm nor deny that I shared with my parents.

interest if they managed my money for me. I can't imagine why. I mean, they only had four-plus years of witnessing my financial irresponsibility to reach this reasonable conclusion.

Obviously, I was shocked and appalled by their irrationality.

They wanted to charge me rent and place that money in an interest-bearing account for when (or if) I moved out. And at 22, I never remotely considered they might have enjoyed my departure as much as I enjoyed my getaway.

Perhaps coincidentally, I also met a girl—whom. based on my 20-something-year old life strategy, I assumed would be my wife since I now had a college degree. I also recently received a promotion at work to a new position, balling for about $30,000 a year. I wasn't going to let a little thing like years of wisdom and parental advice stop me from making a fool of myself. I was 23. Practically a grown-ass man!

Despite my parents' advice, I stubbornly and immediately moved out less than one financial quarter after moving back in.

I got an apartment in town that was only slightly more accommodating than living on the streets and encompassed the approximate square footage of a large moving box.

Less than one month after obtaining my marginally better-than-a-box-with-a-roof excuse for an apartment, my 19-year-old girlfriend of a few months moved across country to live with me. She had no degree and no gainful means of employment. But she was FINE.[15]

---

[15] This translates to "very beautiful," for readers not fluent in millennial slang.

Given my 23-year-old minimum standard relationship requirements, her physical attractiveness more than compensated for her more dire finances.

Since my beautiful but broke significant other didn't have any measurable means of income—something I hadn't considered before she moved in—paying the bills fell on me to figure out. This wouldn't have been so bad if we weren't both high-maintenance, heavy spenders. This may come as a surprise to some of you, but after taxes, $30,000 doesn't stretch very far. Because cutting back on our unnecessary expenses would have made too much sense, I began looking for ways to make more money to cover living outside of our means.

I paid for our extreme spending by doing what I did best: charging everything I could on credit and hoping that The Almighty, or someone equally merciful, would one day come to my rescue. Wanting to help myself in case God was too busy, I had the bright idea of signing up for one of the many consolidation loans I received in the mail every week.

I can confidently say that this was one of the dumbest financial choices I'd ever make.

I don't have anything against consolidation loans. Used correctly, they can be useful tools for helping responsible people manage their money and get on a path towards debt management and eventual debt freedom. At age 23, I was neither responsible nor seriously looking to be debt-free. I had an arbitrary goal of achieving debt freedom by 28 but I had no plan to achieve that goal. That made it about as useful as saying I wanted to own a unicorn by age 28, considering the feasibility of both was equal.

It was more likely for me to get a unicorn. Having never signed up for a consolidation loan, I assumed the loan company would pay off my outstanding credit cards and I would make one loan payment each month for the next 60 months. In a world filled with reasonable people and common sense, this scenario is what should have taken place.

Unfortunately, the only thing that makes sense in this world is the expectation that it will be filled with senselessness.

Once approved, I received a check in the mail for $10,000. Fun fact: mailing $10,000 to someone who demonstrated for nearly a half-decade that they do not know how to budget or manage their money was the equivalent of mailing a blank check.

To my credit, I wasn't *completely* irresponsible. I applied half the check to two of three outstanding credit cards. But in a mind-blowing act of stupidity that I can only reflect on with horror, I used the other half of the check to go on a shopping spree for my girlfriend and me.

Because "we earned it." I have no idea what "it" was we earned, but I do know we spent a lot of money on it.

Proving Einstein's theory of infinite ignorance true, I used the remaining few thousand dollars to put a down payment on a used car. In summary, I doubled my debt burden—barely paying off the original debt—by shifting $10,000 in credit cards to $10,000 in a consolidated loan, the remainder on the original credit card I didn't pay off with the consolidation loan, and now I had a car loan for over $13,000.

For those who can't follow my impressive levels of stupidity, I've tracked it in table form.

Table 1: Debt Before Debt Consolidation

Credit Card #1	$4,000
Credit Card #2	$2,000
Credit Card #3	$3,000
Total Debt	**9,000***

*does not include interest payments outstanding

Table 2: 48 Hours after Debt Consolidation

Credit Card #1	$0
Credit Card #2	$0
Credit Card #3	$3,000
Consolidation Loan	$10,000
Car Loan	$13,000
Total Debt	**$26,000***

*does not include interest payments outstanding

You read that right. In one weekend, I nearly tripled my debt and added a 60-month car loan to my portfolio of financial ignorance. I didn't know it then, but I would spend the greater part of the next eight years paying off debt I accumulated in less than eight hours.

Irresponsibility is a funny thing. You would think the weight of crushing debt would have been enough to stop me, and maybe, if I lived alone, it would have been.

With a financial enabler in my life, I had to keep up faking the funk. So, on an income of $30,000 with $26,000 in debt, I decided the best thing to do was …upgrade to a more expensive apartment.

To be fair, this decision wasn't solely my girlfriend's idea. At any time, I could have pointed out that neither she nor I could afford our lifestyle. However, in an act of misinformed chivalry, I felt it was my responsibility to make sure the bills were paid, even if many of those bills were self-imposed and outside of our means. When she told me she wanted to move to a nicer, yet more expensive apartment across town, I offered minimal protest.

I confess, if you haven't noticed, that I like nice things, too.

Besides, we weren't exactly moving into a McMansion. But when you're broke, every dollar counts. Further, we never bothered budgeting for the very few dollars we had between the two of us to count.

On the bright side, she had a job working at a local bank by this time. On the dark side, we continued the act of lifestyle inflation.[16]

What we failed to realize is that adding expenses every time you get a raise does not a budget make.[17] We lived paycheck to paycheck, and when our paychecks ran out, we lived from credit card to credit card.

Since no immature couple is official until they buy crap they don't need, we also bought some furniture we couldn't afford for the apartment we couldn't afford, along with a new flat screen HDTV we also couldn't afford. For a mere $3,000, I was able to get a "great deal" on the latter purchase by opening an allegedly low-interest loan.

Despite making low money, we were living the high life.

---

[16] When increasing your expenses always manages to outpace your income.

[17] That would also assume we had a budget in place to break, which we did not.

I wasn't even pretending to manage or pay off my debt. I was defeated and happy to make the minimum payments. Now, thanks to the consolidated loan, I could give the illusion of having more money than I did. Never mind the fact that now I owed more people more money.

> **DFDT Tip:** *Remember loans are amortized. For example, depending on your interest rate, the first 10-years (or more) of your mortgage will primarily go to mainly paying down just the interest, taxes and insurance of your total outstanding mortgage balance.*
>
> *Barkrate.com/calculators offers free resources and Excel (Microsoft Office) offers a free "Loan Amortization Schedule" to help you estimate payments, interest, and scheduled payments.*

Perception was reality.

It didn't end there. When we weren't busy buying new things we didn't need, we went to clubs in town or in other cities to waste even more money we didn't have. I was broke, but I'd be lying if I said I wasn't having a great time living the good life.

Like all good parties, it had to come to an end.

With dreams of grandeur, my girlfriend eventually decided that small-town living wasn't going to cut it for the lifestyle she (or we?) needed to live. Fortunately, I wanted to keep her happy. Unfortunately, my job only offered relocation to offices located in Austin, Texas. I grew up in Austin. Like most people who leave their hometown by choice, I vowed never to return.

Austin isn't a bad city, but like any city where you spend most of your life growing up, you're bound to make some friends and some enemies. I didn't have a long list of enemies, but that didn't make me any more eager to return to the place where I had spent ten years of my youth making them.

The prime Austin nightlife, known as "Sixth Street," is one long corridor of decorative bars. I knew I was bound to run into my fair share of ex-girlfriends, ex-guy-friends, and ex-friend-friends. I was doing fine spending and living outside of my means without involving my frenemies, in front of whom I would need to "stunt" even harder to prove how much better my life was than theirs. Despite these red flags, I requested, and received, a job transfer. I notified our apartment manager that we'd be breaking our lease (another fee).

I wasn't thrilled about the process, but at least I had my girlfriend.

I thought.

While I was making tentative plans for our future, my girlfriend was making separate plans for her own future.

A part-time model when I met her, she received an offer to model in New York City. I might have been able to compete with many things, but New York City was not one of them. The decision was simple. She was going to New York, and it came down to whether or not I planned to join her.

For all my cumulative years of ignorance, the idea of traveling across the country with no job and no prospects did not strike me as appealing. Every month I had bills due that I could barely afford even under the most ideal circumstances. I loved her. Love might not cost a thing, but my bill collectors dictated that I *needed* a paycheck.

Even if I did want to go with her—and a part of me did—there was no way I could survive more than 30 consecutive days without a constant, and now higher, paycheck. I had accumulated far too much debt. As a bonus, she lost (quit?) her job before the New York opportunity arose. If I didn't pay our bills, who would?

I don't want to oversimplify the decision-making process. It was very difficult. Yet, basic math dictated that I needed to work, consistently and often. I wasn't going to stop her from going to New York. I didn't even bother to ask her to stay. But there was no way I could go with her.

Since my job transfer was already scheduled, I still had to move to Austin, alone.

Fortunately, I hadn't burned all my bridges back home. I linked up with an old high school friend who, as it turns out, needed a roommate too. Over one weekend, he and I found a reasonably priced place and agreed to split the rent.

We signed the paperwork, and I drove back home to tell my girlfriend the news. As chaotically as we began, we ended. She began traveling to New York more and more frequently before making her final move. During that time, I began planning my transition to Austin. By the time she left for good, I, now nearing 25, was stuck back in Austin. All I had to show for my life since college was a one used car, one big screen TV, and a whole lot of debt.

In some ways, being heartbroken kept me from spending more money. All I did was work, pay bills, come home, and repeat. I was too tired to date. I was too depressed to go out. I was emotionally drained but budget-wise, this was one of the most financially responsible periods of my 20s.

Chapter 3
The Cost of Doing Living

They don't teach you about the cost of living in school. Austin was about three times as expensive as where I previously lived, and I didn't factor in the higher costs' impact on my meager income before the move.

> *DFDT Tip: Having moved half-a-dozen times in my adult life, correctly estimating cost-of-living adjustments are practically a part-time job of mine. For ease of use my favorite calculator is CNNMoney's Cost of Living Calculator. For thoroughness, I like (guess who) Bankrate.com Cost of Living Calculator.*
>
> *I've written about this topic for several outlets; most thoroughly for my own at paychecksandbalances.com/debt-to-income*

Soon, I had to find a second (and sometimes third) job just to cover my bills. In addition to working full-time, I would pick up odd contract jobs in the evenings, weekends, or nights. I did everything from building computers, selling phones for commission, and working nights and weekends at hotels.

Basically, if I wasn't asleep, I was working. If I wasn't working, I was asleep. This was one of the few periods in my 20s that my debt didn't increase. I didn't have the time.

During one of my many random odd job searches, I found a job like my own with a respectable pay increase. Although I was only minimally qualified for the position, I applied anyway, not expecting anything to come from it. Even as I was going through my second- and third-round interviews, I half-expected to be turned down.

To be clear, I liked my current job. I had only been working there for about 12 months but that didn't change the fact that I needed more money, period. It was a good job, but there wasn't a raise or opportunity for promotion.

When the new job called with a firm offer, I jumped at the opportunity. This was the first time in at least three years I began seriously thinking about getting out of debt again. With my new raise, I thought this was as good a time to revisit my consolidation loan offer. I figured with the lessons learned from my first experience, I could negotiate a reasonable rate and make a financial change for the better.

I was half-right.

By 2008, I had over $30,000 in debt from various credit cards, personal loans, an outstanding school loan, and accumulated interest. I hadn't realized how close to the fringes I was living until missing one credit card payment provided an eye-opening experience.

The payment I missed was for one of the first credit cards I'd opened. I accidentally missed the bill in the mail and without warning, my next credit card bill showed an APR of 29.99%. This was over a 300% increase in interest rate in *one* month.

I literally could not afford it. And, with all my other bills barreling down on me, I couldn't afford to make those minimum payments either.

I'd been a loyal customer with this credit card issuer for nearly five years. I figured a simple phone call would correct the issue.

I called customer service that evening. I think I was even in a good mood when the call started. I explained that I had never missed a payment. I was happy to pay the minimum amount and associated fees for both months but there was no way I could continue making payments at a 29.99% APR on an outstanding balance in the thousands.

Their response? I'll paraphrase.

"That ain't our problem."

A series of expletives and name-calling might or might not have followed. But a series of very dumb, very emotionally based decisions followed. I didn't want to do business with them anymore. I knew that. To teach them a lesson, I decided to self-sabotage by making three concurrent and poor financial choices:

First, I demanded they close the credit card immediately. That will teach them, a multi-billion-dollar empire, I thought. In reality, I was hurting myself far more than I was hurting them given that your credit score is calculated based, in part, on how much available credit you have—a fact I didn't know at the time nor one that they volunteered.

Second, using a balance transfer from another card that already had a ridiculously high balance of its own, I transferred the debt. This was an equally misinformed decision because of the standard balance transfer fee, which, although part of a low-interest deal, was likely equal to or higher than the 29.99% APR I was protesting on the original card.[18]

Third, because I both didn't know how nor had I ever budgeted a day in my life, when the next month arrived, I was as surprised as anyone to find out that it would be impossible for me to make

---

[18] It seems I preferred the avalanche method of poor-decision making to the slower snowball effect.

all the new total minimum payments. Five years had passed since I graduated college, but financially, I was in the exact same position as when I left—unable to make minimum payments on my credit card debt.

I had to act and act fast. I had received several consolidation loan offers over the years since my prior epic fail. Paranoia and fear kept me from taking them. Now I didn't have a choice. If I didn't do something in the next 30 to 90 days, I wasn't going to have enough money to pay all my bills.

Panicked, I desperately rifled through my most recent offers looking for the lowest APR. A large, well-known institution's offer stuck out from the group.

For some reason, I trusted this offer. I figured that if a large bank who specializes in making loans for a living was giving me a pre-approved offer, then surely things couldn't be that bad. Otherwise, why would they take a risk on me?

A respectable bank would never extend credit to someone who couldn't manage it, right?

That pre-approved consolidation loan offer gave me a sense of self-validation. My situation couldn't possibly be that dire if banks were still offering me even *more* credit. I just had to get this one last loan, then everything would be OK.

With nothing but hope to guide me, I called the phone number on the front of the consolidation loan. I had no plan or recourse if they turned me down. Failure was not an option. Subconsciously, I knew if this conversation didn't end well I would quickly spiral into a pattern of missed payments that ended in bankruptcy.

I did my best to push those thoughts out of my mind. I tried to sound friendly and unbothered when the loan consolidator answered. I wanted to cry and beg for an offer. By that point, I would have taken anything they gave me.

Several years of juggling my debts was about to evaporate in a mirage of fiscal irresponsibility. I had to get this loan. I was optionless.

I'll never forget the conversation. It would forever alter my financial life.

Today, I understand the loan person was just doing his job. I was probably one of hundreds, if not thousands, of frantic souls he spoke with during his shift. I was down on my luck and we both knew it. It was still tough to listen to the arrogance in his voice as he spoke down to me on the call.

I was placed on hold several times while he entered my information. He'd come back, ask a few questions—none of which I knew the answer to. Questions like, "do you know your credit score?", "do you know your total annual income? Monthly income?", "do you know how much debt you owe each month?"

It didn't matter the question. I think the only answer I got right was my name, maybe. He'd type, then place me on hold, pepper me with another basic financial question I couldn't answer, then place me on hold again.

I assumed that behind the scenes they were calculating whether I was even worth the risk.

More accurately, he was literally calculating my future. I could only hope in silence that he got the numbers right.

As I waited in silence with nothing but my thoughts to haunt me, it dawned on me that the loan company had several options at their disposal. I had none. They could approve me instantly, place my offer in a queue for further consideration, or outright deny me. I was playing a game of Financial Roulette, and only they had the power to pull the trigger.

I hated this game.

There have been few times in my life when I've felt less in control. I was peppered with questions. I had no answers. He hesitated after each response, as if stifling laughter at how poorly my answers were scoring. I was anxious but increasingly agitated.

If they were going to turn me down, I wanted them to just tell me! This was precious time that I could spend wallowing in self-pity and self-medication. My frustration only amused the operator, or maybe I was drowning in my own emotions. After minutes that felt like hours, he came back with a tentative offer.

Both the monthly payment and interest rate were higher than the "pre-approved" offer I had in my hands. Based on the hundreds of APRs I'd seen over the years by then, the rate seemed high, real high. I feigned a weak protest.

Undaunted, the operator explained the facts. He told me "based on our calculations" the company's offer was more than generous. On average, "Mr. Garrett, the interest rate was lower than many of your current credit cards. For example, he one you just closed had an interest rate of 29.99%," he scolded.

He also pointed out that my monthly payments, in total, were higher than the monthly payments they were offering—a fact that I had forgotten to calculate, so I had to assume he was telling the truth. I didn't have my bills in front of me to confirm or deny his assertions. Even if I did, I hadn't made a budget in 25 years of my life, and I certainly wasn't going to develop one in the next 25 seconds.

I realized I could have continued disputing in principle, but it was an effort in futility. He already knew what I was finally starting to realize. I was going to take whatever they offered me that night. I didn't have another choice.

I'd never felt so disgusted with myself. He reminded me that they needed an "affirmative response" before they could move forward.

Verbally acknowledging defeat, I admitted, "I'll take the offer."

"We'll get that right out to you," he said and hung up.

Table 3: Rock Bottom

Credit Card #1	$0
Credit Card #2	$0
Credit Card #3	$3,000
Consolidation Loan	$10,000
Car Loan	$13,000
Flat Screen TV Loan	$3,000
Total Debt	**$29,000***

*does not include interest payments outstanding

Aside from the car payment, I had a new $15,000 loan on the way that would allow me to consolidate almost all my outstanding credit into one "low" monthly payment. If I stayed disciplined, I would make my final payment by age 30. I should have been happy.

Instead, that night was one of the lowest points of my life.

How did I let it come to this? How had I let my debts grow to a point where I couldn't even pay the *minimum* payments? This didn't make sense! I was constantly working. Hell, some months I worked three jobs!

WTF?

I was tired. I was sick. I was sick of being tired.

That night I vowed to never let my debts get that bad again. I hadn't admitted it until then, not even to myself. I had a serious problem.

I reached rock bottom.

My stubbornness made me determined to get myself out of debt. Through my own doing, I had put my fate in someone else's hands. I hated coming to that realization, and I *never* wanted to feel that hopeless again.

For the first time since I received a credit card contract at age 18, and a yo-yo for my troubles, I was unwavering in my resolve to get out of debt.

I had a goal. That was a good start. I still didn't have a plan. That was a big problem.

Chapter 4
How I Dug My Way Out of Debt

Making the decision to get out of debt was one of the easiest things I have ever done. Actually *sticking* to the decision was one of the hardest things I have ever done.

It turns out, spending money and living outside of your means is a lot easier than living a responsible life for a decade. Not only is debt management not fun, it also sucks.

To sweeten the deal, getting out of debt takes *a lot* longer than it does to accumulate it. In my case, it would take three times as long to get completely out of debt as it took to get into debt.

Most people have a linear path to debt freedom. Not me. I tripped, stumbled, failed, pushed, and sometimes outright stopped on my journey to debt freedom. Each time, though, I started back more determined than ever. Usually motivated by remembering that debt consolidation loan phone call I had made at age 25.

"Never again," I'd repeat to myself.

During the first part of seriously pursuing debt freedom, I simply had a goal: I wanted to be debt free. This was a goal. I often confused it with having a plan.

They are not the same.

A goal without a plan is about as useful as dreams to an insomniac. At least I was motivated, even if I didn't have a clear path to success. It turns out that even misguided direction is sometimes better than no direction at all.

While I had been working several odd jobs over the years, I accepted that working one job wasn't going to bring in enough income for me to hit my debt-free goal. Instead of working contract jobs on a freelance basis, I began applying for part-time jobs I could do on the weekends in addition to my full-time job. I put my pride aside and accepted that maybe, despite my college degree, I wasn't going to get rich working a 9 to 5.

Lottery winnings notwithstanding, I needed the combination of two (or possibly three) incomes if I wanted to pay off my debts in my lifetime.

I'm sure there were plenty of options I could have chosen. Instead, I chose a part-time sales job with a major phone carrier because they were the first employer to call. Luckily, the company also paid a decent hourly wage, plus commission. Had I been more responsible, I might have completely paid off my debts in a few years by simply allocating all my part-time paychecks toward my debts.

However, despite all that I had been through, responsibly spending and budgeting continued to be a difficult lifestyle for me to adopt. I took the more mature but slightly less advisable route of allocating the majority of my part-time job's paychecks to my debts, but not all of it.

I was maturing, but I was by no means mature.

Even when you have the "scared straight" moment in your life, old habits die hard. I used my new extra cash to revisit those old habits. Between the depression from breaking up with my ex and working all the time I hadn't gone out much since returning to Austin.

I took this influx in cash as an opportunity to correct this injustice. I took vacations, and essentially reinstated my fiscally irresponsible life. The only redeeming quality, which is admittedly pitiful, is that I didn't use my credit cards to fund these adventures. I finally had cash.

So, while I was still being irresponsible with my money, I was no longer funding these extravaganzas on credit. Between bottle-popping, random trips, and occasional dabbles in relationships of varying seriousness, I managed to put a dent in my outstanding debt.

Despite these moderate accomplishments, I forgot to take into consideration one key factor: I was getting older.

When I was in my early 20s, working 50 to 80 hours a week and sleeping four to six hours a night barely registered. As my early 20s gave way to my late 20s, exerting myself for 24-to-48-hour periods without sleep had a detrimental impact on my ability to function. My age, coupled with the excessive partying and drinking during what few off hours I did have, began to take its toll on my performance at my day job.

I had to choose.

I didn't have the energy or the willpower to continue working two or more jobs for the rest of my life even if it was helping me manage my debt.

After realizing this, I quit my second job so I could focus on my main job. This decision meant I quickly went back to living check to check. Fortunately, the small dent in my debt I had made with the part-time jobs allowed me to live slightly above my means on one paycheck. But I still had no savings, so I was always one paycheck away from spiraling back into crippling debt. I was constantly subject to the real possibility of burning through my credit cards if I ever lost my job or if anything went wrong.

DFDT Tip: An emergency fund turns an emergency into an inconvenience. The "experts" recommend saving three to six months in an emergency fund, but even as little as $500 in savings can be a huge difference maker. In fact, <u>two economists studied 70,000 households</u> and found about $2,500 is the magic emergency savings number.

Unless something changed, I realized that I might need to live with a roommate for the rest of my life. Despite the life-changing revelations of my mid-20s, I was no closer to owning a home, buying a car, or doing much of anything that would demonstrate I was progressing from being a menace to society—and a menace to myself—to a fully-functional, positively contributing adult member of society.

Due to the volume of my past poor decisions, I was either going to have to work two jobs again or look for another job if I wanted to make any significant progress. And with these debts hanging over my head, I felt like I wasn't ready to pursue a serious relationship. A part of me didn't want to burden anyone else with my self-created financial problems. Furthermore, I was in some ways scarred by the way I managed my money the last time I was in a committed relationship. In my mind, there was no way I could manage myself, money, *and* a relationship at the same damn time.

Looking back, this mindset was unfair. I projected my poor money management experience with one woman to how I might manage my money with *any* woman. This narrow-minded thinking made me assume a successful relationship could only occur *after* I learned successful money management skills. In other words, I convinced myself I had to get out of debt *before* I could make other positive changes in my life, including being in a serious relationship.

I don't know if it was the best choice or not. It was the choice I made and the one I had to live with. At the expense of all other pursuits, even love, I made debt management my singular focus.

To assist, I began looking for a singular job that might help fund my expenses. Opening myself to possibilities across the country, I began looking for work that offered a higher fixed income.

As with most of my well-intentioned, half-assed ideas, I thought my job search would take years given the fact that I began looking for jobs at the beginning of what would later become known as the Great Recession (2009). Yet, as was my luck with most poorly thought-out plans in my life, I received a call back for a job offer in Denver, Colorado less than four weeks later based solely on a phone interview. It came with a generous[19] pay increase.

To this day, since I didn't account for a cost-of-living adjustment, I continue to wonder if everyone simply broke even on that salary "negotiation." Assuming you consider negotiating me asking for a number I thought sounded cool and them immediately agreeing to it.

To spice up the uncertainty of the unplanned move to a city where nobody knew my name, the job came with a six-month mandatory probation during which could be fired without cause or explanation at any time and for any reason during that six-month period. Which meant that I would be moving to a state I'd never lived to work in an office I'd never seen with the possibility of being laid off in less than six months in the middle of a recession.

---

[19] I think.

Then there was the matter of my relationship. I had a girlfriend who I would need to break up with or take with me, which likely meant we would need to get engaged.

And to top it all off, I still had roughly $30,000 in debt and no Texas-based plan to pay it off.

Despite how intimidating it felt to move to Colorado, my past choices left me with no choice in the present.

In the end, I put in a two-week notice with my job in Austin and sold everything I owned that wouldn't fit into a used Toyota Camry. Less than six weeks and one 13-hour road trip later, I moved to Colorado.

Alone.

****

As some of you already know, or I hope you never experience, debt is a burden that can change the trajectory of your life, personal and romantic relationships, and lived experiences. While this is one of few personal stories I share in this narrative, it is only one of many examples where past debts kept me from moving forward. I hope today's decisions don't become tomorrow's ghost for you either.

However, I ask that you forgive the abruptness of the transition here. I wanted to acknowledge without minimizing the emotional impact this decision had on myself and the lives of others, while also remaining respectful of my and their personal lives. The brevity of this story isn't a reflection of the lack of the gravity of the situation. Instead, it is meant to leave out specific details simply out of respect to the personal lives of the people involved.

The remaining sections transition towards focusing on how to get out of debt. My intent is to provide you all with a road map that may hopefully prevent you and others from having to ever face difficult choices like choosing between money, debt, or love. In an ideal world, those aren't definitive choices we should have to face.

You should want to have your cake, and another cake too.

Chapter 5
D. - Define the Problem

J ust because someone offers you credit does not mean you know how to responsibly manage it. Just because you can buy it, doesn't mean you can afford it.

In my mid-20s, despite never making more than $9/hour during college, I had amassed well over $30,000 in available credit by the time I graduated. This meant I had the ability to spend $30,000, plus interest, before I secured my first job out of college making $20,000 a year. Given all my financially frivolous adventures, it is amazing I didn't max out all my credit cards.

The Lord works in mysterious ways.

When I was younger, I figured that banks were knowledgeable institutions that would never extend more credit to me (or anyone) than I (or they) could afford to pay back. I believed that for the five years I attended college, which, as we've established, provided me with no personal finance skills to be able to survive in the real world. Instead it was the real world that taught me Personal Finance 101.

I recommend you **do not** follow in my path.

One lesson that took me far too long to learn was to define the totality of my debt. Adding up all your debts in their entirety is something I suggest you do at the beginning of your debt-repayment journey rather than midway or at the end like I did. If you have a lot of debt, determining how much isn't as easy as you might think.

For this reason, I recommend you begin by requesting your credit report. This will give you a factual accounting of all your debts rather than relying on your flawed memory, which will usually round the debt numbers down and in your favor.

By federal law, you are entitled to at least one free credit report from all three major credit bureaus each year. You can read more information about the law and access your report through the Federal Trade Commission's website at https://www.ftc.gov or directly at AnnualCreditReport.com.

Your Credit Report

Your credit report and credit score Credit Score are not the same.

Both contain many of the same factors, but they are two independent reflections of your credit history and creditworthiness to lenders.

Credit Report

Your credit report reflects your credit activity and history for at least the last seven years and may extend as far back as ten years for certain circumstances. This report includes a summary of where you lived, how consistent you've been in paying your loans and debts, if you've ever been sued, and whether you've ever filed for foreclosure or bankruptcy. It also provides information on accounts in good standing or past due, your various credit limits compared to the outstanding balance, and the number of accounts you have open.

Your credit score is not included in your credit report.

The three major nationwide credit reporting agencies -- Experian, Equifax, and TransUnion -- collect and maintain your history in their national databases. With your approval, these credit reporting agencies can sell your information to legally approved creditors, lenders, insurers, employers and others looking to evaluate your credit history. Therefore, your report might have a direct impact on your interest rates, mortgage rate, rental approval, credit card rates and approvals/denials, or even an employer's decision to extend you a job offer. It could even affect other things like insurance offers, cable TV, or utility and cell phone deposit requirements.

You can review your own credit report for fraud, identity theft, or inaccurate credit reports from lenders. Federal law legally entitles you to your credit report every 12-months from the three major credit reporting bureaus.

CTA 5.1: Visit the official website for ordering your **free** credit reports at AnnualCreditReport.com (or complete the Annual Credit Report Request Form and mail it to: Annual Credit Report Request Service, P.O. Box 105281, Atlanta, GA 30348-5281). For even more information visit the Consumer Financial Protection Bureau (CFPB), a U.S. government agency that makes sure banks, lenders, and other financial companies treat you fairly.

Credit Score

Your credit score is calculated based on your credit report. There are hundreds of credit scores available to you and your lenders. If interested, you can order your credit scores at MyFico.com. It is my opinion that you **should not** pay for your credit score, but I wanted to make you aware that the option exists. As of the date of this publication, you can obtain a **free** credit score from most credit card issuers and several apps like Mint and Credit Karma now provide it for free as well.

Your credit score may vary based on the reporting agency that provided the information, with the most frequently cited being Experian, Equifax, and TransUnion. Because the credit bureaus are competitors, your credit score may vary based on the proprietary calculating methods used by each company. This "scoring model" is a unique formula used by the companies to calculate your individual credit score. Be aware that the loan type you're applying for or even the day the score was pulled may influence your final score.

Several items might impact your score including payment history, total unpaid debt, and the number and type of loan accounts you have open. For example, secured loans like mortgages are typically viewed more positively than credit card debt. Other factors like your total available credit, new applications for credit, and your credit utilization rate (total debt owed divided by available credit) also impact your score.

Each factor does not affect your credit score the same. According to Experian, a typical FICO score will consider:

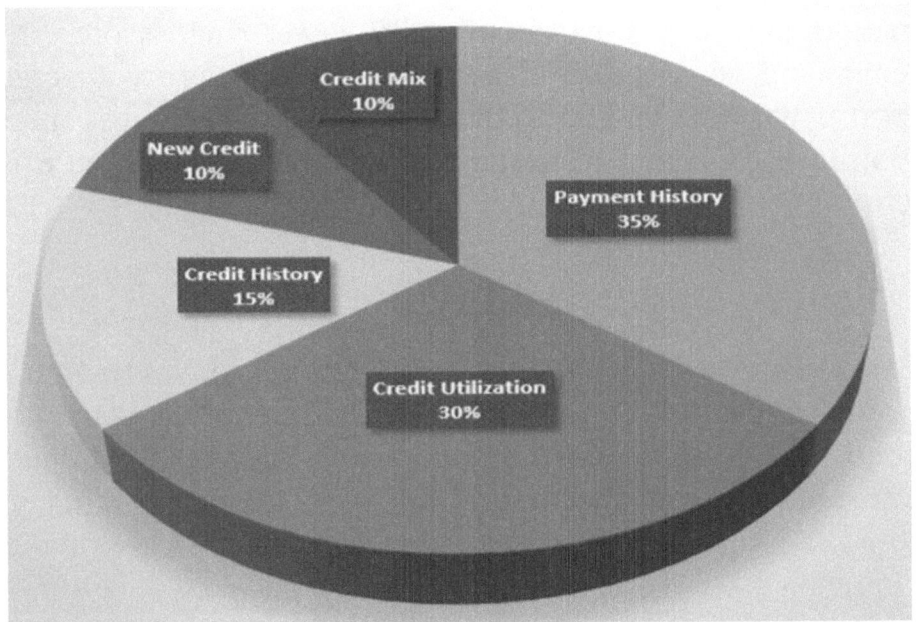

- Payment History: 35 percent

- Debt Ratio (how much you owe compared to your available credit limit): 30 percent

- Credit History (age of credit usage): 15 percent

- New Credit: 10 percent

- Mix of Various Types of Credit: 10 percent

Most credit scores range between 300 to 850. A high credit score (typically 740+) indicates a positive payment history and can make you eligible for lower interest rates on loans. It might also remove the need for a deposit and indicates you've been a responsible consumer with other lenders and services. Basically, a higher credit score reflects your creditworthiness, is a strong indicator to lenders that you are low risk, and you have a higher likelihood of paying back your debts consistently and on time.

Credit report errors can artificially lower your score, so I recommend you check at least annually to ensure your credit report is accurate and up to date. You can correct most simple reporting errors online through each of the main credit bureaus' websites.

Understanding Your Debt

This section will focus on credit cards and student loans (mortgage loans will not be covered). To better understand your debt, there are some basic definitions we'll cover for frequent terms found on your statements. This is not all inclusive but will provide a foundation for you to learn and change how you view your debt.

Your Credit Card Statement

If you bank online, most information can be accessed from your lender's website or mobile app. Stated simply, the Terms & Conditions define all the legal terms you agree to when taking on the debt. Paychecks & Balances guest, Wilson Muscadin, said we should "view every transaction you make with a card as a loan agreement."

I never viewed debit and credit cards this way before. Wilson's philosophy helped me gain a better appreciation for the Terms & Conditions. Like most people, I willfully sign but typically ignore the contractual terms. I **highly recommend**, as painful as it may be, **you read every word (also known as terms of service)** for any and all debt you take on, especially school loans and loans you plan to cosign for a spouse, friend, or family member.[20]

The following covers a non-exhaustive list of key terms you'll find on your statement that you should focus on month-to-month and "red flags" to pay even closer attention to.

A. **Minimum Payment Due** - The amount you **must pay** by the Payment Due Date.

B. **CTA 5.2**: A best practice is to pay off your bill in full each month. If you have debt, set a goal to at least pay a little more than the minimum payment. This action is how you maintain a healthy credit score and reduce interest ("interest charged") payments.

C. Previous Balance - If applicable, this reflects your outstanding balance owed from the previous month.

D. New Balance - Amount owed as of the statement close date. This is the amount of credit you have used plus any fees and interest charges for the month.

E. **Payment Due Date** - If the minimum payment due is not received by this date, then interest will be assessed. If missed, most creditors will charge both a late fee on your next bill *and* increase your interest rate on **all** outstanding balances on the account.

F. **CTA 5.3**: Always pay the *Minimum Payment Due* by your account(s) **Payment Due Date**. Failure to make at least the minimum payment will lower your credit score, cost you a late fee of up to $35 or more, and in many instances, raise your current APR on **all** outstanding balances to as much as 29.99% APR or higher.

---

[20] PaychecksAndBalances.com - What Happens to Your Debt After Death?

G. <u>Fees: Finance or Interest Charges</u> - All associated costs for any fees, finance, or interest charges accumulated during this month's billing cycle.

H. **<u>Credit Limit</u>** - Your credit limit or credit line is your card's spending limit. Interest, pending charges, and fees may further reduce your available credit.

> Credit Line Available - this is the amount of available remaining credit. However, this isn't always displayed on all credit card statements. It is typically easily accessible for most online accounts.

CTA 5.4: Limit your credit utilization (your new balance divided by your available Credit Limit) below 30% whenever possible. While maintaining a zero balance and paying in full each month is the goal, no more than 10% utilization is reasonable. A utilization rate over 30% can start to negatively impact your credit score.

I. <u>Cash Advances: and Balance Transfers</u> - a summary of the amount of Cash Advances and Balance Transfers charged to your account and the associated Interest Charges for the month. Many lenders charge high interest rates on cash advances (and Balance Transfers after the promotional period ends). In addition, most lenders apply your Minimum Payment Due to lower-interest-rate balances to maximize overall interest rate charges to you and profits for them (No, this is <u>not</u> illegal.).

J. <u>APR</u> - The annual percentage rate (APR) is the annual rate charged for borrowing (charging your purchases on credit) expressed as a percentage for the actual yearly costs.

<u>Credit Cards - Key Sections</u>

- Account Summary - As the name implies, this section will summarize your transactions cover such terms as those covered above like: Previous Balance, Payments, Credits, Fees, Interest, Credit Limit, and more. This may be broken out into subsections like "Payments, Credits, and Adjustments" and/or "Standard Purchases" or "New Charges". When applicable, Fees, Interest, Advances, and Balance Transfers may be reflected in this section.

- **CTA 5.5:** Make sure all information is accurately reflected, paying special attention to any Payments and Credits (returns, pending balances, payment holds, etc.) you believe should have been accounted for or dropped during the month. Unexplained charges might be fraudulent, and you should contact your lender or 'dispute' immediately online to start the research and review process.

- Payment Information - If not already covered in the Account Summary, the Payment Information section will state a list of payments individually made throughout the month. It may also list any Credits that apply.

- Account and Contact Information - If you didn't read those Terms & Conditions when you signed up, this section will contain a summary of information, such as: your lender's contact information, legal disclosure, how your interest is calculated, your rights, and other information, like how to update or change your mailing address.

This is not an exhaustive list, and the order or categories may be reflected with slight differences on your statement(s).

CTA 5.6: For exact details, review your lender's site (either reviewing a PDF, electronic, or physical credit card statement) to see if they provide a "How to Read My Credit Card Statement" or Frequently Asked Questions (FAQ) for a specific breakdown of your lender's statement. If you ever have questions about your statement, do not hesitate to contact your lender(s) directly.

Credit Cards - Red Flags

It is important that you review your Credit Card Account Summary and Payment Information in detail each month. However, there are some "red flags" where you can pay close attention for errors or concerns.

- **Late Payment Warning** - This section will cover the late fee and APR increase that might be applicable if you do not make the Minimum Payment Due by the Payment Due Date. You might face penalties, fees, and interest rate increases as high as 200% or more!

- **Minimum Payment Warning** - This section will briefly cover how long it will take you to pay off your debt only making the minimum payment versus how quickly you will pay off the balance in 36-months and the interest saved. An analysis by Chase Bank found a credit card holder with a balance of $2,000 on a card with an 18% APR could save thousands in interest and cut as much as 11 years off by simply adding an additional $10 to their Minimum Payment Due.

Credit Cards - Researching and Choosing the Best Credit Card

Most people wait for a credit card offer to come in the mail and sign up with minimal research. This is a passive approach and doesn't ensure you have the best credit card for your lifestyle. If you need or want a credit card, I recommend an active, well-informed, lifestyle-based approach to choosing your next card.

Nowadays, there are several sites you can use for **free** to find the card that will work best for you based on your credit score, rewards, purchasing history, annual fee, and much more!

CTA 5.7: Before signing-up for your next card, use aggregate sites like NerdWallet or CreditCards.com to find the card best suited for your needs. I recommend not applying for more than one card at a time and if rejected, no more than once every three months. Keep in mind that a hard credit check **will** temporarily impact and lower your credit score; however, it's better to conduct an informed search than to sign up or apply for random offers you receive in the mail.

Student Loans

For the class of 2016, the average student loan debt was over $37,000. At a conservative rate of 6% interest for a 25-year repayment plan, a typical student would owe more than $34,000 in interest alone and need to cover more than $71,000 in total debt payments ending in the year 2041.[21]

This scenario assumes the student makes every payment on time with no unexpected life events resulting in a late payment, penalties, or deferment over a 25-year period. That would put these students well into their 40s and 50s, and it's hard to assume that no unplanned events will occur during that time. Most students will apply for some type of loan. And if that loan isn't enough to cover the cost of college, many also use private loans, federal loans, or other sources like credit cards to fill the gap. Students and parents should keep in mind that school loans must be repaid whether you graduate, pause your schooling, or drop out.

---

[21] Bankrate.com/calculators

Reducing college costs, not a great student loan rate, is the most crucial focus to helping a family or individual maintain healthy personal finances.

Some means of reducing college costs might include earning as many credits as possible during high school, obtaining credits from a local university or community college before transferring to your dream school, or considering attending a lower-cost university before transferring to (and graduating from) your first choice. The key is to minimize your college costs and associated school loans.

There are other considerations specific to whether you choose a private or federal loan (or combination).

- **Federal:** Federal loans are based on individual student needs and household income, among other factors. Like any other loan, there are pros and cons to consider for this funding source.

- **Private:** In most cases, private loans are used by students and parents to bridge the funding gap for any college costs not covered by federal loans. However, in some instances, a family may need to completely cover the cost of college using private loans and other funding sources. There are pros and cons of private loans as well.

If you must use all or school loans to fund your education, these red flags should be taken under careful consideration.

Student Loans - Red Flags

With the clarity of age and hindsight on my side, I remember several occasions when I was spending my "free" credit card money and my friends were right beside me spending their "free" school loan refund checks. Decades later, many of us are still paying off these balances plus interest, so let me be clear: **School loan refund checks are not free!**

There are few scenarios where living on your student loan (not to be confused with your scholarship) money is a smart decision. The scenarios are so few, I can't think of any, but I've heard a few individuals tell me in very rare circumstances it makes sense. However, for the purpose of this book, if you ever use your student loan to purchase a non-essential (food, water, shelter), you are making a poor financial decision that will financially haunt you for years to come..

Student loans should be avoided if possible and if not, should be used as minimally as possible since any funds you use you will have to repay after you graduate. Scholarships, grants, and other funding sources such as part-time income are a far better option to student loans.

I recognize that for many individuals and families, school loans are the only means of covering the cost of a college education. In this instance, I again emphasize that you take the lowest interest options available, and you take funds for **needs** only. Student loans should not be used for wants or luxury amenities or purchases.

CTA 5.8: Read your school loan package in its entirety. Parents, this includes you. You need to review the loan package for any forms or documents you sign, since you may also be committing yourself as a co-signer. A co-signer promises to cover the loan in the event a payment is **ever** missed.

CTA 5.9: Equally important, I highly recommend all parties use a school loan calculator to understand the **full costs** of your student loan(s) before signing your contractual agreements. While Excel offers several free loan amortization templates you can use to estimate your loan costs and total interest, you can find online resources at sources like: FinAid.org's Loan Calculator, BankRate's College Planning Calculator, and the Repayment Estimators available through the U.S. Department of Education's Federal Student Aid website.

Student Loans - Other Considerations and Refinancing

As with any debt, or loan, you should always try to pay more than the minimum each month if you can afford it. This is an easy way to start paying down the principal and not just the interest.

Other Special Considerations (Federal vs Private Loans)

If you have federal loans, or use a mix of federal and private loans, there are additional considerations you should consider *before* refinancing your federal loans. While some federal loans might have higher interest rates than the refinancing offers, you're considering they also have special protections that you will be giving up if you refinance with a private loan company.

For example, if you are in or looking to enroll in the Federal Public Service Loan Forgiveness Program (PSLF), there are several restrictions that *do not* apply to private loans. Specifically, the act of refinancing may make you ineligible for PSLF. Additionally, if you are currently enrolled in any federal student loan repayment plans specific to your federal loan(s), you may no longer be eligible to continue your plan under your new agreement.

CTA 5.10: Before renegotiating or refinancing *any* federal loan, you should consult with your federal loan holder(s) first to understand what, if any, implications it will have on your debt, contractual agreement, or any other special repayment services you are currently using. In some instances, these protections are better than the low-interest refinancing payment plans you are considering. Using one of the student loan calculators listed above might show that you'll pay *less* over the lifetime term of the loan without refinancing.

Refinancing Your Student Loan

The availability of historically low interest rates and increasing competitive business practices in the financial industry has led to an unprecedented spike in companies competing for student loan repayment services. The better your credit score (740+), the more options you'll have to refinance your student loans at lower rate, provided you have no other consumer debt. Remember, these companies are in the business of making money. They may lower your interest rate, but it's still up to you to do your due diligence, maintain responsible spending habits, and above all else, protect yourself at all times.

These refinancing companies generally fall into two categories: Traditional and Peer-to-Peer.

- **Traditional**: Traditional methods of refinancing your school loans includes using institutions like banks, credit card issuers, and credit unions. These institutions have been around for decades and typically look to refinance your loan for a lower interest rate. More recently, credit card issuers like Discover have begun marketing low-interest rate offers for student loans. Typically, you will simply need a good-to-excellent credit score (740+) to get the best rates and if you qualify, the refinanced loan will completely pay off your previous lender.

- **Peer-to-Peer**: Although not a new idea, Peer-to-Peer lenders (P2P) have spiked in popularity for student loans and other debt repayment services in recent years. P2P is the pooled lending of money by investors for a service, in this instance, student loans. P2P lending may be offered as a traditional loan or a refinancing option. This is a growing market, but popular companies as of the date of this publication include SoFi, Prosper, Lending Club, and many others. This might be an excellent route for new or returning students to find low-interest or competitive loan options or for graduates looking to refinance.

If you are considering refinancing a federal loan with a private loan, remember that you might lose some of the protections that come with federal loans. Carefully weigh whether it's worth losing those simply for a lower interest rate.

Chapter Calls to Action

1. Visit the official website for ordering your **free** credit reports at AnnualCreditReport.com (or complete the Annual Credit Report Request Form and mail it to: Annual Credit Report Request Service, P.O. Box 105281, Atlanta, GA 30348-5281). For even more information visit the Consumer Financial Protection Bureau (CFPB), a U.S. government agency that makes sure banks, lenders, and other financial companies treat you fairly.

2. Best practice is to pay off your bill in full each month. If you have debt, set a goal to at least pay a little more than the minimum payment. This action is how you maintain a healthy credit score and reduce interest ("interest charged") payments

3. Always pay the **Minimum Payment Due** by your account(s) **Payment Due Date**. Failure to make at least the minimum payment will lower your credit score, cost you a late fee of up to $35 or more, and in many instances, raise your current APR on **all** outstanding balances to as much as 29.99% APR or higher.

4. Limit your credit utilization (your new balance divided by your available Credit Limit) below 30% whenever possible. While maintaining a zero balance and paying in full each month is the goal, no more than 10% utilization is reasonable. A utilization rate over 30% can start to negatively impact your credit score.

5. Make sure all information is accurately reflected, paying special attention to any Payments and Credits (returns, pending balances, payment holds, etc.) you believe should have been accounted for or dropped during the month. Unexplained charges might be fraudulent, and you should contact your lender or 'dispute' immediately online to start the research and review process.

6. For exact details, review your lender's site (either reviewing a PDF, electronic, or physical credit card statement) to see if they provide a "How to Read My Credit Card Statement" or Frequently Asked Questions (FAQ) for a specific breakdown of your lender's statement. If you ever have questions about your statement, do not hesitate to contact your lender(s) directly.

7. Before signing-up for your next card, use aggregate sites like NerdWallet or CreditCards.com to find the card best suited for your needs. I recommend not applying for more than one card at a time and if rejected, no more than once every three months. Keep in mind that a hard credit check **will** temporarily impact and lower your credit score; however, it's better to conduct an informed search than to sign up or apply for random offers you receive in the mail.

8. Read your school loan package in its entirety. **Parents, this includes you**. You need to review the loan package for any forms or documents you sign, since you may also

be committing yourself as a co-signer. A co-signer promises to cover the loan in the event a payment is **<u>ever</u>** missed.

9. I highly recommend all parties use a school loan calculator to understand the **full costs** of your student loan(s) before signing your contractual agreements. While Excel offers several free loan amortization templates you can use to estimate your loan costs and total interest, you can find online resources at sources like: FinAid.org's <u>Loan Calculator</u>, BankRate's <u>College Planning Calculator</u>, and the Repayment Estimators available through the U.S. Department of Education's <u>Federal Student Aid website.</u>

10. Before renegotiating or refinancing *any* federal loan, you should consult with your federal loan holder(s) first to understand what, if any, implications it will have on your debt, contractual agreement, or any other special repayment services you are currently using. In some instances, these protections are better than the low-interest refinancing payment plans you are considering. Using one of the student loan calculators listed above might show that you'll pay *less* over the lifetime term of the loan without refinancing.

<u>Additional Recommended Reading</u>

For an even more detailed analysis on how to define your personal finances, I recommended *Your Money or Your Life* by Vicki Robin, Joe Dominguez, Monique Tilford. You can read my review at <u>PaychecksAndBalances.com/Books</u>.

Chapter 6
E. - Establish a Plan

When I decided to become debt-free, I picked an arbitrary age - 28 - because it was simple and five years from when I made the decision. Other than that, I had no plan, so from the beginning I was planning to fail.

Predictably, I failed.

Why?

I never calculated how much I would need to pay to be debt-free in five years. I simply said I wanted to be debt-free and I assumed I would my way to success.

Do. Not. Think. Like. Me.

To succeed, you need to set a reasonable goal accompanied by a plan or system to help you achieve that goal. You will also need a realistic timeline, so you don't spend five years working two or more jobs only to realize that, at the end of those five years, you still have $20,000 of debt.

Unreasonable timelines and no plan only set you up for failure.

While the no-plan plan is preferred because it requires no measure of success or failure, and in most cases, no action, it does not set you up for success sooner than later. It sets you up to procrastinate until the end of time. And what's waiting for you at the end?

More debt.

Setting a timeline forces you to evaluate whether your current income, salary, and budget will allow you to succeed. This is assuming you're honest with yourself. If you can't be honest, visit Bankrate.com/calculators and use their calculators instead.

CTA 6.1: If you want to establish a debt-free plan that will work, you need to **set a timeline** *and* pick a **budget system**. We'll walk through the details of how to do both later in this book.

Find the Appropriate Debt Calculator

There are two main tools you need for your D.E.B.T Free plan. One is a debt calculator. The other is consistency.

Most people don't know how much debt they owe. Coupled with your credit report, a good debt-free calculator can help you estimate your total debt, interest owed, and help you clearly understand the impact of paying over the minimum payment.

You only need one calculator. I'm biased towards Bankrate's resources, but I don't care which debt-free calculator you choose, as long as you use a good one.

CTA 6.2: Choose **one** Debt-Free Calculator

- **Bankrate.com**
    - Bankrate.com/Calculators (All Calculators)
    - Multiple Debt Types
    - Credit Card Only
- **Vertex42.com**

    - Debt Reduction Calculator

CTA 6.3: Choose <u>one</u> Repayment Plan from either the 'Traditional' or my 'D.E.B.T. FREE' options shown below.

Traditional Debt-Free Repayment Plans

Once you've got an understanding of your debt and how much you can afford to pay over the minimum each month, you can determine which debt repayment strategy or system will work best for you. Two basic methods are most widely known: the Debt Avalanche and the Debt Snowball.

Although I never personally applied either while paying off my debt, I'll briefly describe both since they have worked for many people.[22]

1. **Snowball** - You pay off your debt from your smallest to largest balance. Remember, you **continue to make minimum payments** on all debts, but any extra money is put towards your smallest balance.

2. As each debt is paid off, you roll or "snowball" these funds towards paying off your remaining balances in order of smallest to largest until you are completely debt free.

3. **Avalanche** - This method is more difficult to follow because it takes longer to see a financial benefit. However, it does save you more money on interest payments in the long run.

With the Avalanche system, list your debts in order, starting with the one that has the highest interest. That's the one you pay off first, moving on the next highest interest rate and so on until you are completely debt-free.

---

[22] Just $10 a Month Could Save You 11 Years and $1,600 in Interest Payments – PaychecksAndBalances.com

Reminder: no matter the system, always **make the minimum payments** on all debt. You don't want to miss a payment and have to deal with the consequences of that.

Studies show people are more likely to stick to the Snowball method, or any plan, that allows them to see their debts paid off faster. In other words, most people like to see their debts at $0, and the Snowball method allows you to see your debts at $0 the fastest.

D.E.B.T. Free Repayment Plans

There are thousands of different ways to pay off your debt. I used four, and for the purpose of this book, I'll cover the methods I used in chronological order. However, I'll also quantify the difficulty (easy to hard) of each versus their effectiveness (low to high). Unfortunately, the easiest to implement is not the most effective, but I believe they all helped me progress towards my goal, so I'll share them all. As you might expect, I chose the easiest route before finally arriving at the most difficult, yet most effective, choice. You may need to do the same.

I suggest you challenge yourself but also suggest you use the strategy that gives you the greatest chance of success. And if you find one isn't working for you, change it up. **Adjust the plan, not the goal.**

Repayment Strategy #1: Pay off debt with "whatever is left"[23]

    Ease of Implementation: Easy

    Effectiveness of Paying off Your Debt: Low

---

[23] If you're as habitually irresponsible as I am, there's rarely anything left.

Strategy: As the name implies, this strategy involves taking whatever sum of money you have left before your next paycheck and applying it towards your preferred debt(s). I say preferred debt because this "strategy" is not strategic. It's a starting point.

Table 4: Whatever is Left

Description	Amount
Debt	$10,000
Interest Rate	15%
Minimum Payment	$200*
Extra Payment	$0
Total Interest	$15,851
Total Debt + Interest	$25,851

* Each payment strategy assumes a minimum payment of 2% of your outstanding debt. Your lenders may charge more or less. This information should be available on your credit card statement or contract.

There are several reasons why this strategy is ineffective. First, if you're already in debt, you probably don't have much disposable income between paychecks. In other words, you're literally living paycheck to paycheck. High interest rates on the credit cards or loans you might have compound this issue (no pun intended). Even if you have low interest rates, you likely have high balances. In a worst-case scenario, you have both high interest rates and high balances. Therefore, this strategy is the equivalent of throwing a stone in the ocean. While it might create ripples, there is minimal effect on your total ocean of debt.

I only began using this strategy because I was doing nothing to pay off my debts, and I wondered what would happen if I did something crazy like pay more than the minimum payment some months. This first foray into paying off my debts gave me a taste of what it was like to see my balance go down versus up each month. Still, there were far more moral victories than actual victories.

The only benefit to this strategy is that if you keep at it long enough, you might be able to free up enough money to begin using a more effective debt repayment strategy like the ones described below.

Repayment Strategy #2: Pay the minimum balance plus a set dollar amount.

Ease of Implementation: Easy

Effectiveness of Paying off Your Debt: Low

Strategy: Like Strategy #1, this plan doesn't take much work since most of the math is done for you. You simply take the minimum balance required on each of your credit cards or loans and pay more. You can do this one of two ways.

First, you can choose one card or loan to focus on, which is what I recommend. Second, you can tackle all your open credit cards and loans if you have the available means. Just remember the goal is to start driving down one or all your balances by making a set payment that is larger than the minimum balance due each month.

Table 5: Minimum Balance + Set Payment

Description	Amount
Debt	$10,000
Interest Rate	15%
Minimum Payment	$200*
Extra Payment	$25**
Total Interest	$4,688
Total Debt + Interest	$14,688

* Each payment strategy assumes a minimum payment of 2% of your outstanding debt. Your lenders may charge more or less. This information should be available on your credit card statement or contract

**Calculations assume you pay this fixed extra payment until debt free.

While Strategy #2 is more effective than Strategy #1, the main issue is that you still haven't defined a timeline for your end goal. In addition, how much over the over the minimum payment you make will be driven by the amount of money you *feel* like paying each month rather than a predetermined, fixed amount.

This strategy is limited by how effective you decide to make it. Put simply, if you pay more, you'll pay your debt off quicker. If you pay less, it will take longer. Since feelings are rarely as consistent as logic, this strategy tends to vary in effectiveness. Therefore, as soon as you can, you should begin moving towards repayment strategy #3 or #4.

Repayment Strategy #3: Pay a randomly-set dollar amount.

Ease of Implementation: Moderate

Effectiveness of Paying off Your Debt: Moderate

Strategy: This strategy is where you'll finally start making a real difference in paying off your debt. I rank this strategy as "moderate" because its success depends completely on you. It could easily be considered highly effective—minus one key component that I'll cover in Strategy #4—if you decide to make substantive payments each month.

Table 6: Minimum Balance + Randomly Set Payment

Description	Amount
Debt	$10,000
Interest Rate	15%
Minimum Payment	$200*
+ Randomly Set Payment	$50**
Total Interest	$3,950
Total Debt + Interest	$13,950

* Each payment strategy assumes a minimum payment of 2% of your outstanding debt. Your lenders may charge more or less. This information should be available on your credit card statement or contract

**Calculations assume you pay this fixed extra payment until debt free.

The goal with this strategy is to determine a fixed amount of money you can live without each bill cycle. I say, "bill cycle", but using your bill's due date isn't the most effective method to use. Rather, I recommend you make a payment as soon as you have the money. If you have $1 dollar more than you need for essentials, then apply that $1 dollar immediately to your debt. If you have $10,000 extra[24], pay $10,000 immediately. Trust me. It

---

[24] I'm impressed.

will always be more difficult to spend money you don't have access to than it will be to wait until that bill's due date.

For example, if you get paid on the 1st but your bill isn't due until the 31st, that is 30 whole days when you'll have to be responsible enough to spend your money on the bill rather than, well, anything else more fun than paying bills. You would need exceptional resolve. Let's be honest. You're already in debt. If history is any indication, do you truly believe you have the resolve to hold on to money any longer than 24 hours, let alone 30 consecutive days?

Probably not.

But you might find yourself wondering how much money you should spend on debt each month. The answer is there is no wrong answer. You're striving for progress, not perfection. However, one of the easiest ways to determine how much money you should allocate towards debt is to use that debt repayment calculator again.

You'll also need to consult your budget. If you don't have a budget, you need to develop one. I don't have a specific recommendation for a budget calculator but there are plenty of apps to choose from. If you're not comfortable with apps, Excel or Google Sheets works just fine, as does a regular 10-key calculator, a pencil, and a piece of paper.

Don't make creating your budget complicated. You only need an estimated budget to establish a framework for this specific strategy. It doesn't have to be exact. Of course, the more accurate your budget the more helpful it will be to you, but don't become paralyzed by analysis if your income fluctuates. Even an informed guesstimate is better than having no budget at all.

The idea behind this is to determine how much extra money you have each month to put towards your debt. All you need to come up with a rough debt payment estimate is how much money you make each month on average (total income), how much money you owe others (total bills), and how much you commit to miscellaneous expenses, including entertainment and fun (discretionary expenses).

Your budget should look something like this:

Total Income – Total Bills – Discretionary Expenses = Discretionary Income

See, nothing fancy. But now that you know your "Discretionary Income", you can do one of two things. First, you can allocate 100% of your discretionary income to your debt repayment plan (this is what I recommend). However, if you're just getting started paying off your debt, this is incredibly difficult to implement. It's hard to go from making only minimum payments to spending all your disposable income on debt. It leaves you feeling deprived and frustrated and leaves little room for motivation to keep going.

Which means that the second approach to this strategy is to allocate a fixed portion of your discretionary income each month to debt repayment and gradually cut back on things you don't need to eventually reach that 100% threshold. In other words, start by paying what you're comfortable with and then increase from there.

Yes, it sucks to give up Netflix or your boutique gym membership or your social life now, but you're not doing it in vain. Each dollar you allocate to debt repayment will get you closer to your goal of debt freedom.

While the previous three strategies have their pros and cons, Strategy #4 is by no coincidence the most difficult and most effective strategy. In its simplest form and most convenient definition, this strategy is another variation of all the above strategies, combining all their best attributes. It also factors in the most critical variable: TIME.

Repayment Strategy #4: Pay a fixed dollar amount based on a fixed debt payoff timeline.

Ease of Implementation: Hard

Effectiveness of Paying off Your Debt: High

Strategy: You'll notice that unlike most debt payment books, nowhere in this book do I cover a roll-up, roll-down, or roll-anywhere strategy. That's because I think none of those things really matter. There will always be better, faster, or quicker methods of accomplishing your goals, but none of them will matter if you constantly quit.

What I have found is the most important strategy for debt freedom success is to **pick a plan that you can follow**. It doesn't matter if you follow this book, a different book, blog, article or tip from a friend, stranger, or expert. If it works for you, follow it. The plan that works for you and is tailored to your goals will, in my opinion, always be the most effective.

The key difference between strategy #4 and the other strategies I've outlined is time. There's a saying that a goal without a timeline is a fantasy. I try not to be pessimistic, but when it comes to debt management, the truth of that statement is inescapable. Time is waits for no one. Adding something as simple as a time-specific goal to your plan forces you to succeed or fail.

Here's an example of why time is so critical for the success of any debt repayment strategy.

Table 7: Minimum Balance + Fixed Payment

Description	Amount
Debt	$10,000
Interest Rate	15%
Minimum Payment	$200*
+ Extra Fixed Payment	$200**
Total Interest	$2,065
Total Debt + Interest	$12,065

Each payment strategy assumes a minimum payment of 2% of your outstanding debt. Your lenders may charge more or less. This information should be available on your credit card statement or contract.

***Estimated example of extra payment (increase or decrease to adjust for your available discretionary income).*

In the four "$10,000 in debt" examples above, paying $200 over the minimum payment gives you 33 years of your life back and saves you almost $14,000 in interest payments!

In this case, time can work for or against you.

To see how it can work for you, use an app or debt repayment calculator to define when you want to pay off your debt and exactly how much money you need to pay each month to achieve your goal.

The mistake most people make when tackling debt, present company included, is never accurately calculating how long it will take to do so. With an indefinite timeline, most people will give up, fall off, or fail completely. I cannot emphasize enough how important defining exactly when you want to be out of debt will be for helping you reach your goal. It might take one year or ten years, but at least now you know.

Once you've chosen a time frame and exact amount of debt, you'll need to pay each month, all that's left is simultaneously the easiest and most difficult part: stick to the plan. It really is that simple and that difficult. Assuming you don't run into any major hardships, changes in APR rates, or increase your debt while attempting to pay off your existing debt, you will succeed.

If based on the budget you created, you're still unsure how to allocate your discretionary income to the above payment strategies, you can use this rule of thumb: use whatever money is available from your Living Expenses (needs) and Entertainment (wants) budget to expand as follows:

- **Conservative:** Add an additional 10-25% of your budget towards debt payments by making an equal decrease from needs and wants cutbacks.

- **Moderate**: Apply an additional 25-50% towards debt payments.

- **Aggressive**: Apply an additional 50-75% towards debt payments.

You may be shocked by these numbers, or even think they're impossible to reach. **They are not**.

Remember, almost 60-70 percent of the average household budget goes towards funding just three expenses: housing (33%), transportation (16%), and food (13%). Focus your cutbacks in these three areas to have the biggest impact on your overall budget.

I didn't own a home but I cut back on living expenses (smaller apartment and a roommate, when appropriate), paid off my *used* car, and stuck to a strict budget for food, mostly by cutting back on eating out and preparing meals at home and using leftovers for lunch at work. Towards the end of my journey these changes helped me find almost $1,500 per month.

Was it fun? Nope. Did it take lots of sacrifice and discipline? Yes. Was it worth it? Also, yes. You can change the plan, but never change your goal: **D.E.B.T. Free.**

Chapter Calls to Action

1. If you want to establish a debt-free plan that will work, you need to **set a timeline** *and* pick a **system.**

2. Choose **one** Debt-Free Calculator

   a. **Bankrate.com**

      i. Bankrate.com/Calculators

   b. **Vertex42.com**

      i. Debt Reduction Calculator

3. Choose one Repayment Plan from either the 'Traditional' or 'D.E.B.T. FREE' options found in this chapter:

Traditional:

   a. Snowball

   b. Avalanche

D.E.B.T. Free options:

   a. **Repayment Strategy #1:** Pay off debt with "whatever is left"

   b. **Repayment Strategy #2:** Pay the minimum balance plus a set dollar amount

   c. **Repayment Strategy #3:** Pay a randomly-set dollar amount

   d. **Repayment Strategy #4:** Pay a fixed dollar amount based on a fixed debt payoff timeline.

Additional Recommended Reading

Establishing a (good) plan is the most important part of a successful D.E.B.T. Free journey. In order of preference, I recommended the following reads to further increase your odds of success: *The Millionaire Next Door: The Surprising Secrets of America's Wealthy* by Thomas J. Stanley; *The Automatic Millionaire* by David Bach; and *I Will Teach You To Be Rich* by Ramit Sethi. You can find my full up-to-date list and reviews of each read at PaychecksAndBalances.com/Books.

Chapter 7
B - Build a Budget

You will have to make sacrifices. Lots of them. For example–and I know this might be the equivalent of asking you to volunteer to drown to death–you might even have to give up the following non-exhaustive list on a *temporary* basis: name-brand everything, cable, the latest smartphone, new music, etc.

I'll put it in simple terms: If you're spending money on anything non-essential to your survival, give it up. You're wasting money on instant gratification when that same money could be used to get you completely out of debt forever. That's a lifetime of gratification.

To make sure there is no confusion, I'm defining "non-essential" as anything that doesn't contribute to your ability to maintain access to food, water, and shelter. Don't confuse your wants for needs, just because you *really* want it.

I know it sounds terrible, and I speak from experience. I gave up all these things for a few years. I wasn't complimented on my clothing or expensive dates for a long time. I was called cheap more often than I can count, but you know what?

It was all worth it. That's was it took to be debt-free, and that's what was important.

Marcus' First Budget

When I finally developed a budget, I was 27 years old. I realized I had taken on significant lifestyle creep. If you're not familiar with that term, it's the phenomenon where every increase in pay relates to an increase in purchases. This is a recipe only for living paycheck-to-paycheck until you check out.

Once I realized this, I made some simple changes that had a significant impact on my ability to pay off my debt. Lifestyle deflation rather than reckless spending looked like this for me:

Table 8: Lifestyle Deflation[25]

Expense	Approximate Monthly Savings	Annual Savings
Rent (roommate)	$300	$3,600
Food (eating out less)	$100	$1,200
Cable (canceled)	$200	$2,400
Miscellaneous	Various	$1,000
Total		**$8,400**

Before I decided to get out of debt, I never had a budget. My budget planning consisted of spending until I ran out of money and figuring out how I was going to make it to my next paycheck.

I was surprised how little changes could save me thousands of dollars a year. In addition to the practice of tracking my money, which helped me better manage my money, short-term sacrifices led to amazing long-term gains. In the table above, for example,

---

[25] Miscellaneous: For years, I gave up new cell phone and electronic purchases, name-brand clothes, and yes, haircuts ($20 a week x 4 a month = $960/year). I also cut back on discretionary spending on stuff like movies, coffee from a chain that shall not be named, etc.

the simple act of not having cable for five years meant I saved $12,000 ($2,400 annual savings x 5 years) on an expense I self-selected to maintain. It's not that I don't like cable; I do. I just prioritized paying off my debt. There is nothing on TV worth $12,000.

Resist the need for instant gratification. You deserve better, and you don't have to change much to get it.

Choose a Budget System

You know why you want to create a budget. Now you need to choose a budget or system that you'll actually follow. Below are some of my favorites. Review each of these budget types then choose the **one** most closely aligned with your lifestyle, goals, wants, and needs.

CTA 7.1: Due to the importance savings should have in every budget, I recommend you **pay yourself first**.

This means the 'Retirement, Debt Payments, and/or Savings' category -- found in each system below -- should always be given priority. If you don't have 20% to immediately allocate, then try starting with the maximum amount you can save. Even if it's only 1%, save that. One percent is greater than the 0% you are currently saving.

Whenever you have extra cash, roll it into the 'Retirement, Debt Payments, and/or Savings' category. Optionally, if or when you receive a raise each year, you can roll this amount towards your savings. For example, if you receive a 2% raise each year, consider moving the 2% into your savings fund each year until you reach 20%.

Once you've chosen a system, I would stick to this budget for at least **one full month**. If it works, continue using or updating it as your lifestyle changes. If it does not work, try choosing another budgeting strategy or take a weekend to purposefully review why it didn't work. Based on this information, choose another budget system or combine the strengths (leaving the weaknesses behind) with another system that aligns better with your lifestyle. Continue repeating this exercise until you have a budget system in place that works for you **every** month (ok, most months).

To get started, you'll need to figure out your income and expenses. This can be as simple or detailed as you want. You can review your monthly expenses from the last three months to estimate your expenses. If your income is variable, average the last three months to come up with a reasonable estimate. If you need additional help, refer to my free budget tool (download a **free** PDF at DebtFreeOrDieTrying.com/Budget) I created based on a breakdown of where most Americans spend their money.

Remember, the average American spends 70% of their income on three expenses: housing, transportation, and food. In fact, in most major cities, roughly half of that 70% goes towards paying for your housing and transportation costs. Therefore, any reduction in these three areas will have significant benefit to your opportunity to have more savings month-to-month.

CTA 7.2: Choose One of the Following Budget Systems

The 80/20 Budget

- Life: 80%
- Retirement, Debt Payments, and/or Savings: 20%

This is one of the simplest proportional budget systems available. If this is your first time creating a budget, this one usually works best. Put simply, you save 20% of all income and the remaining

80% of your money is spent however you like. Just remember to include your debt repayment when planning your spending.

The 50/30/20 Budget

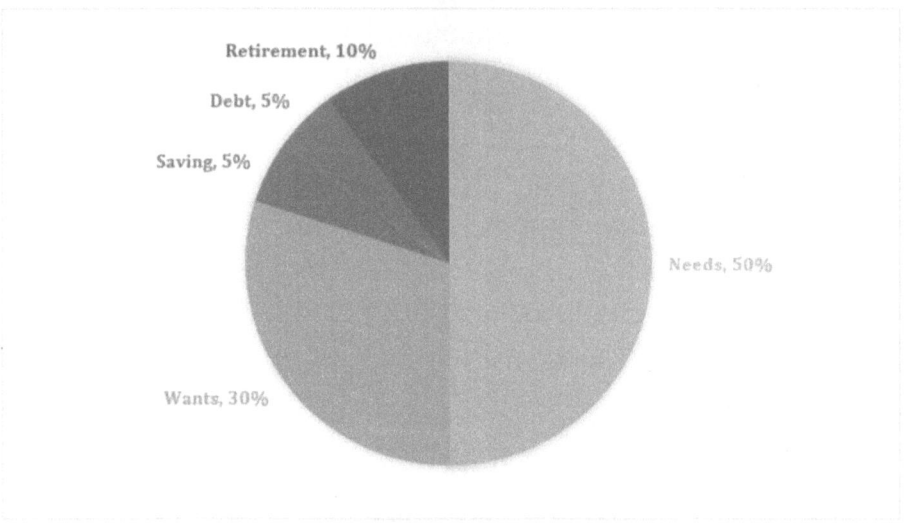

- Living Expenses (Needs): 50%
- Entertainment (Wants): 30%
- Retirement, Debt Payments, and/or Savings: 20%

This is one of my favorite budget systems. If you want to try it out, a NerdWallet article I was featured in, How One Man Dug Out From $30,000 in Debt, has a **free** automated 50/30/20 Budget tool. You can also visit PaychecksAndBalances.com/Best-Budget-Calculator for this budget app and to see all the personal finance tools we have made available from our partnership with NerdWallet.

I prefer this budget because it is simple and allows maximum flexibility for Entertainment (wants). I maintain a fairly strict budget, but I also don't believe in budgetary confinement, where sticking to my budget is such a miserable experience, I hate myself and the budget by the end of each month. I prefer using a budget I will follow versus a budget I know I will actively ignore.

In this scenario, living expenses (50%) include housing, utilities, food, transportation, and other fixed payments that you need to survive. Please do not confuse your monthly survival needs with your daily wants. For example, you want cable. Whether you *need* cable is debatable (not really, it is not a need).

Entertainment (30%) covers personal spending, or what experts call "fun." Do not double-count your entertainment and living expenses here or congratulations, you played yourself, word to DJ Khaled.

Lastly, 20% of your budget is for retirement, debt, and savings. I use this order because even if you live forever, you'll probably still want to retire eventually. Given that retirement is a non-negotiable "when" versus a negotiable "if," then I think you should probably save for this inevitability.

The major key here is to remember that the 20% should be dispersed to one or all these three sub-categories within the 20-percent. In other words, if you have 6 months set aside for savings and you're debt-free, that does not mean you move 20% to another category. It means the entire 20% is allocated towards your retirement account(s).

Note: Some estimates show retirement savings may need to be as high as 22% for Millennials.

The 60/20/20 Budget

- Living Expenses: 60%
- Entertainment: 20%
- Retirement, Debt Payments, and/or Savings: 20%

This is a nice mid-level budgeting system. None of these budgets are particularly complicated, but you can see that a lower percentage is allowed for entertainment in the 60/20/20 Budget. Maybe you're on the wrong side of 30 or maybe you just don't go out as much because you're mature, refined, and own many distinguished leather-bound books. In either scenario, you've decided that your living expenses are more important than Entertainment.

The 70/20/10 Budget

- Living Expenses: 70%
- Entertainment: 10%
- Retirement, Debt Payments, and/or Savings: 20%

When you usually see this budget, it typically defines "Retirement, Debt Payments, and/or Savings" with specific breakdowns of: 10% for retirement; 5% for emergencies, and 5% for debt. This system ensures you're addressing these categories in specific amounts rather than making it arbitrary.

I pull entertainment out as its own category in any budget I use. Frankly, I might accidentally spend all my money on entertainment since it's the most fun category to spend, so I like to specifically track it. That's why my 70/20/10 Budget may look slightly different than some others you've seen.

This budget works best for those looking to repay their debt but have mouths to feed other than their own. As you can see above, most of your income (70%) is allocated to living expenses – housing, transportation, family costs, etc. which makes sense if you have a family or other people who rely on you. Living expenses increase with the more people you need to take care of.

And I know 10% for entertainment is tight but that's the point. You'll need to find expenses you can cut back on such as cable, restaurants, dining out, and discretionary spending to make this budget work, but it can be done.

The Envelope System

- Living Expenses: Envelope(s)/Automate (40-60%)

- Entertainment: Envelope(s)/Automate (20-40%)

- Retirement, Debt Payments, and/or Savings: 20%

This system is popular for several reasons. One, since it's cash-based, you can see exactly where your money is going as you spend it, and it can help you see where you tend to overspend. If you have trouble controlling your spending in general or you habitually charge too much on debt and credit cards, this might be the budget for you. Two, you control your envelope categories. Popular ones include dining out, clothing and shoes, books, and beauty, but you can decide for yourself what works for your situation. And three, it forces you to stick to your budget since you can only spend what's in your envelope. **However, for this system to be most effective, you must be a disciplined individual**.

Like most tools, this system will only work as well as you use it. Don't use the tool incorrectly, then declare the system doesn't work.

Each envelope, automated or physical, should be used **only** for the category you designate. If you spend under, you can roll that money towards personal rewards (covered in more detail later) or you can apply it as a bonus to that category the next time you fill your envelopes.

I recognize that most people don't like carrying or have access to cash 24-7. Further, in some instances, pulling out cash might cost you **more** money if you're charged an ATM fee or need to maintain a certain balance in your account month-to-month. **If you're already disciplined**, but you don't want to carry physical cash, most online banks allow you to create sub-accounts that you can personalize and label. These is sometimes referred to as an "electronic envelope system."

You can use physical envelopes or set up these "electronic envelopes" online to better track and ensure you don't overspend in your various expense categories. Optionally, you can use an app or limit your "envelope" to only those expense areas you struggle in the most. For instance, when I use the envelope system, I usually only withdraw cash for my Entertainment envelope, since this is the area, I'm most likely to overspend in from month to month. Doing so keeps me disciplined, focused, and ensures I don't exceed my monthly goal.

Bonus: Do You Struggle to Budget?

Clearly Differentiate Your Needs versus Wants

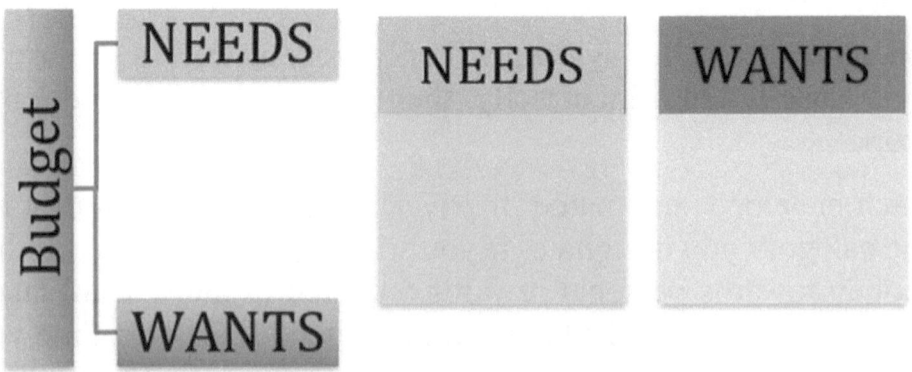

For what it's worth, a surprising revelation for me has been people's inability to disguise their Needs versus their Wants. Specifically, most people consider everything they want to be a need. **This is inaccurate**.

However, I cannot tell you what your own needs and wants are. I am not a psychologist. If you are unfamiliar, you may want to refer to "Maslow's hierarchy of needs" to develop your list. For clarity in this book, my perspective is that a *need* is limited to food, water, and shelter. Another way to view this is that every *want* beyond this very limited list is a want and/or luxury. If you can live (or not die) without it in your life, then it should not be listed on your Needs list. This perspective would slightly change the visual to include the following.

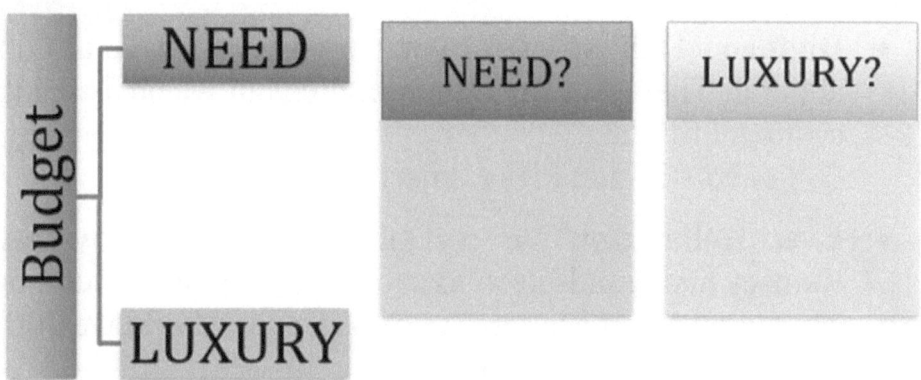

<u>Budget Apps & Automated Tools</u>

I still believe in using pen and paper for budget tracking, but I'm old according to most internet comment sections. Two of my most frequently referenced tools are still a basic income and expenses budget list I maintain in my phone's Notepad and a cheap dry erase whiteboard calendar that I use to track all my monthly bills. All the technology in the world has failed to supersede the success rate of these basic tools.

When I'm feeling fancy, I might even use the **free** templates available from Microsoft Excel. If you want something slightly more sophisticated, I don't blame you. But, don't let the sophistication of the tool act as an excuse for you not to follow your own budget. **The best tool is the tool that works**.

There are plenty of apps that will help you automate your budget. This is not an exhaustive list of the personal financial apps available, but it is a list of apps I have either personally tried or have received good feedback from people I trust.

- **Mint.com** - web-based and mobile app designed to help manage your money, pay your bills, and track your credit score. It's not perfect but it *is* free and simple and my primary budgeting app.

- **Digit.co** - Digit saves for you, so you don't have to think about it. There is a small monthly fee but we analyzed the cost/benefit at PaychecksAndBalances.com/Ditching-Digit and still think it's a smart choice.

- **EveryDollar.com** - EveryDollar is developed by Dave Ramsey and brands itself as a tool to help you "Focus Your Money on What Matters" to beat debt and build wealth.

- **YouNeedABudget.com** - combines easy to use software with Four Simple Rules to help you quickly gain control of your budget, get out of debt, and save more money faster! YNAB is a fee-based service but they do offer a student discount and, at the time of this publication, a free 34-day trial.

Chapter Calls to Action

1. Due to the importance savings should have in every budget, I recommend you **pay yourself first**.

2. Choose **One** of the Following Budget Systems

   a. 80/20 Budget

   b. 50/30/20 Budget

   c. 60/20/20 Budget

   d. 70/20/10 Budget

   e. The Envelope System

Additional Recommended Reading

- My favorite read on budgeting and why we fail to succeed is *Dollars and Sense* by Dan Ariely and Jeff Kreisler. You can find my review at PaychecksAndBalances.com/Books.

Chapter 8
T - Trust the Process

The most difficult part of getting out of debt was stopping my self-sabotaging. Before I finally accepted how bad the problem was, I had already managed to get myself into tens of thousands of dollars of debt. Even worse, other than a used car, I had not a single asset to show for it. Don't get me wrong. I had a great time funding a decade of my life with credit cards. Even a few of my friends have great stories because of my reckless spending.

What was my reward?

DEBT.

After college, I wasn't even 23 years young and already had more than $26,000 in debt. And I wasn't even done! It would be another two years, and thousands of dollars later, before I finally made the decision to get out of debt. The only thing crazier than how long it took me to choose to stop living outside of my means is that no one was ever going to stop me. The decision to stop was my responsibility. That choice is your responsibility, too.

Taking responsibility for your spending habits will be one of the most difficult and most important decisions you make before pursuing a successful debt freedom plan. Until you are serious about getting out of debt by any means necessary, you will fail.

Once you accept that reality, you're more than halfway there. That first step is one step most people will never take. Seventy-five percent of the battle is mental. Make the choice to be debt-free no matter what it takes, then embrace your decision and do whatever needs to be done.

Implement your plan with a tremendous amount of patience. You will not get out of debt overnight. Depending on the amount of your debt, it will take a long time. The sooner you accept this fact, the easier the already difficult journey will be.

On a related note, I'm not a fan of getting out of debt with a group of friends. If you are going to use a 'groupthink' strategy for tackling your debt, **I recommend you use strangers before friends or family.**

> *DFDT Tip: Our like-minded individuals looking to improve their finances are available at Facebook.com/PaychecksAndBalances.*

You might be asking, "Why?"

There is an "I" in credit. In many cases, debt is accumulated on an individual basis (school loans, personal loans, credit cards, etc.). Therefore, sometimes getting out of debt might be easier to tackle on your own, rather than with a team. For instance, have you ever been on a diet with a group of friends or a loved one? When, or if, they fall off the diet, isn't it more difficult for you to stay disciplined?

Debt repayment is similar. It doesn't have to be a team sport. If you or someone else in the group falls off first, it'll make it harder for you to stay focused and disciplined. Getting out of debt is already difficult. You want to minimize any opportunity to 'fall off' the wagon and maximize opportunities to 'stay on'.

If you're not careful, others' failures will give you an excuse to fail, too. If you are going to team up with a group, I suggest partnering with strangers instead of friends or family. Working with strangers can create a friendlier, more positive and competitive environment without the bias or jealousy that comes with family and close friends.

Either way, choose the group dynamic that sets you up for the highest chance of success.

While I'm not against a shared goal, most people need someone objective to keep them strong-willed and focused. If you and your friends have not demonstrated the resilience needed to stay debt-free in the past, then your immediate peer group might not be the best influence in the present.

Please note that I'm not discouraging working in groups. I want to see you succeed whether that means setting a team or individual plan.

Failure is Always an Option

Unless you're perfect, you will fail while you are on your debt-free plan. Expect it. Embrace it. Then, get over it. Because failure *is* an option.

Failure builds character and makes the taste of victory, which you will achieve, even sweeter. It sounds cliché, but the beauty of getting out of debt is that you will succeed simply by never giving up. You didn't get into debt overnight. You won't get out of debt overnight. If you set up a sound and reasonable plan, which the final part of this book will help you do, then debt freedom is inevitable.

If getting out of debt was easy, everyone would do it. The easiest route to a debt- free life is to avoid getting into debt in the first place. Since you're reading this book, I'll assume you didn't follow that plan. That's OK. The first step is recognizing you have a problem.

Now, let's fix the problem.

Chapter Call to Action

When it comes to debt management, if you want permanent changes, you must make lifestyle changes that will stick. If you want temporary benefits, make temporary changes.

Stick to Your Plan, Unless the Plan Needs to Change

I recommend checking your credit score no more than once every one to three months. Several services exist now that will show your credit score every 2.5 seconds. This constant monitoring is pointless. Once you've implemented a sound plan, let it flow naturally. Checking your credit score every hour on the hour will do nothing but drive you crazy.

You only need to monitor your progress, ensure everything is accurate, and that no fraudulent charges exist (these are rare). As your debt decreases, it will reinforce what you're doing and make sticking to your plan easier. Remember, paying off debt is a temporary sacrifice to reach a permanent solution.

During your journey, you will be your greatest ally. You will also be your worst enemy. I hope this book is one of many successful steps you've chosen to take in the right direction. It is through your own determination that you will become debt free or die trying. You can do it. Following the D.E.B.T. Free 4-step plan outlined in this book, you will do it.

Chapter 9
Establishing, Building and Repairing Your Credit

If you've missed payments or defaulted on your debts, you may need to rebuild or reestablish your credit history (approximately 15% of your credit score). Surprisingly, I only missed one credit card payment in my entire life, and this was by accident (I didn't check the mail in time), but I was lucky. It could have been much worse, and there are some things I wish I had known. But now that I do know them, I'll share them with you so you can apply them and make your D.E.B.T Free journey even easier.

Credit Rate (APR) - Request a Lower Rate

My advice here is simple: It never hurts to ask.

You have everything to gain and little to lose, since the worst they can say is no. If you already have a decent credit score (730+) and a responsible payment history, you might already be in a good position to negotiate a lower credit rate. In my experience, like rent, over time my credit APRs have ever gone one direction: up! But I have successfully requested and received a reduction in APR simply by asking them to review my account, especially on cards where my balance is $0, or I recently paid them off.

As your credit score improves or you zero out an account, you should consider asking for lower APR. At best, you might be able to realize hundreds or thousands in savings on your outstanding debt. At worst, you've wasted your time on a phone call.

If you're not sure where to get started or what to say, here's a simple script:

> "Hello, I've recently been reviewing my credit history. I see that my credit score is *insert your credit score here*. Can we discuss options for lowering my APR rate today?"[26]

The operator should be able to take over from here. Remember, you're here to lower your credit score, not **be talked into a sales pitch or new lines of credit**. Take good notes during the phone call.

For instance, write down the date and time you called, who you spoke with, and the terms you agreed to. Later, make sure you review your next statement to verify that the credit card issuer did **exactly** what they promised, such as change the rate on your account **and nothing else**. If not, you need to call back to find out why. This is when your notes will come in handy.

Establishing and Building Positive Credit History

Some individuals have no or limited credit history. If you haven't used credit cards or only have school loans, you may consider establishing a positive and more diverse credit profile by using some of the following.

Note: I am **not** recommending you open several credit cards for the sole purpose of building credit. Having a positive payment history may become helpful when you negotiate large purchases, such as a car loan or home. Proactively demonstrating you can

---

[26] If your income has increased since opening the card, this is a great opportunity to request that your profile be updated. You can also usually update this information online, if you prefer. Maintaining an up-to-date profile might result in a lower rate, better offers from the same lender, or an increase in the available credit line available to you.

responsibly manage multiple debt types can result in low-interest rates on purchases where a few percentage points can result in thousands of dollars in saved interest.

If you don't want to use or can't gain approval to traditional credit cards, consider the following options:

- **Credit Builder Loan** - Use a credit builder loan to establish both credit and savings. Offered by many online lenders or your local credit union(s), a credit builder loan allows you to borrow money that you can claim as you own once it's paid off. The additional benefit is the loan payment is reported to the credit bureaus on your behalf.
- **Secured Credit and Debit Cards** - Typically, a secured card's credit line is directly tied or equal to the deposit you make with the card issuer. For example, including upfront fees, a deposit of $500 grants you a secured card with a limit of $500. You can use this card to demonstrate habits of positive purchasing and monthly pay off. If you don't like or want credit cards, this is a great low-risk alternative to a traditional credit for increasing your credit score or establishing credit history if you have none. As with any credit card, don't forget to do your research. Use aggregate sites like NerdWallet or CreditCards.com to find the secured card best suited for your needs.

Debt Settlement and Debt Consolidation

Most individuals start receiving credit card offers when their credit score is around 600 or greater. Honestly, these offers are usually awful. The good credit card offers start coming when your score reaches 700 with the best offers usually being withheld for those with excellent credit (750+). Keep this in mind as you begin exploring options to rebuild or repair your credit.

Whenever possible, I highly recommend you avoid high-interest credit cards until your credit score reflects your positive repayment history. Once you've raised your credit score, you may want to consider the following options:

- **Debt Settlement** - A mistress by many names, debt settlement may also be referred to as debt arbitration, debt negotiation or credit settlement. The main purpose of debt settlement is for you and your creditor(s) to agree to a negotiated amount (settlement) less than the outstanding balance(s) that all parties agree will _fully_ satisfy your outstanding debts. This method typically, even if temporarily, lowers your credit score since this information will usually be reported to the credit bureaus by your lender(s). This is not meant to discount the pursuit of Debt Settlement if you still feel it is the best option for your current circumstance. This guidance is simply meant for you to keep in mind before engaging a debt settlement company on your behalf, since some individuals are surprised when their score, even if temporarily, goes down before it goes up.

- **Debt Consolidation** - In full disclosure, I have used debt consolidation on multiple occasions from several large banking institutions and the P2P lender SoFi. That said, when I am ready to be responsible, I have found debt consolidation to be the easiest, most straight-forward method for me to either lower my interest rates, centralize all of my payments in one place, and/or pay off my debt. The primary difference between settlement and consolidation is that consolidation is one (or more) loans provided to you to pay off many other loans or debt whereas settlement is simply an agreement with the lender regarding your payment amount.

You can find Debt Settlement and Debt Consolidation offers through both traditional options like banks and credit unions, or P2P markets such as SoFi, Prosper, Lending Club, and many others.

My final piece of advice before choosing either alternative is to do your research. Equally important is to do a "gut check." I recommend these only as the last option if you are <u>serious</u> about finally paying off your debts.

<u>Chapter Call to Action</u>

As with any debt service, be sure to read the contract in its entirety and ensure you are aware of any processing fees, loss of protections, or prepayment penalties that might come with the new loan. You can always follow up with a representative for any questions or misunderstandings you may have **before** signing any loan or co-signing contract.

Remember, it is your responsibility to understand the loan and all its repayment repercussions.

<u>Additional Recommended Reading</u>

The most comprehensive book I have read on credit scores and how they are calculated is *Your Credit Score: How to Improve the 3-Digit Number That Shapes Your Financial Future* by Liz Weston.[27]

---

[27] Listen to our podcast interview with Liz Weston at PB56: The Truth About Credit ft. Liz Weston.

Chapter 10
D.E.B.T. Free - A 4 Step Plan

We've reached the close out, the part of the journey where the DJ starts playing Journey's "Don't Stop Believin'" or Semisonic's "Closing Time".

When I was buried in debt, I thought being debt-free was a claim I'd never make. It seemed hopeless. I know now that it's not.

I also realize now that sometimes debt is unavoidable. Sometimes it is inevitable. Other times, debt is self-imposed accidentally or with purpose. One of the main reasons I wrote this book is to inspire others to see that they can get out of debt no matter when or where they begin their debt free journey. As you begin, traverse, or end your journey, please remember the four steps that helped me.

Finally, if you enjoyed this short read please do me a favor by leaving a 5-star review on Amazon or Goodreads. This small step provides me with much needed feedback, will allow me to further improve and revise future editions, and helps inform potential new readers. Most importantly, the residual royalty payments will allow me to continue to drink dessert wine...and keep my light bill paid.

For the latest updates on where I am speaking, training, or generally engaging with the public, visit TheMarcusGarrett.com.

About the Author

Born and raised in the Great State of Texas, Marcus obtained a bachelor's degree in business after surviving the mean streets of the inner suburbs. Since that time, some of the nicer names he has been called include freelance writer, blogger, author, auditor, financial analyst, and most relevant to this book, "debt free."

There are myriad details related to his upbringing, but most importantly, Marcus Garrett was founded in the Millennial start-up year of 1982. According to questionably reliable data, yet repeatedly published in the news so it must be true, Millennials – and therefore Mr. Garrett -- use sarcasm as a self-coping mechanism, have average education yet grandiose self-esteem buoyed by unchecked ego inflation and years of unearned participation trophies. What he lacks in focus he more than makes up for with misplaced discipline.

The exhaustive shortcomings of his generation are amplified by a sense of entitlement, apathy, narcissism, and a need for constant praise and affection. Tragically, these many faults do not even include the untold but undoubtedly negative effects of rap music and the Internet.

Mr. Garrett is too indifferent to correct what might very well be misplaced assumptions about himself and his peers. Therefore, he spends most days humbly expanding upon his vast collection of participation trophies while meandering through life unencumbered by either debt, burden, or worry about anything that extends beyond the length of his nose. When he is not passively working, you can find Mr. Garrett on various social media platforms passionately offering a plethora of unsolicited opinions.

A decade of audit experience in fields as diverse as criminal justice, law enforcement, and health care combined with freelance writing on topics ranging from current events to love and relationships helped him develop a uniquely qualitative and quantitative writing style. The *Debt Free or Die Trying* series keeps readers entertained with a combination of cautionary scared-straight tales and helpful tips for staying out of debt or getting out of debt.

Marcus is ardent about serving others and looks forward to identifying more ways to support people who can relate to his story with managing, reducing, and paying off their debt through continued efforts at:

- TheMarcusGarrett.com
- DebtFreeorDieTrying.com

www.ingramcontent.com/pod-product-compliance
Lightning Source LLC
Chambersburg PA
CBHW030712220526
45463CB00005B/2008